Transitions
"My Journey Towards Living a Purposeful Life."

by
Dr. Charles A Kelly
Copyright © 2020

Unless otherwise indicated, all content is licensed under a Creative Commons Attribution License. All Scripture quotations, unless otherwise stated, are taken from The Holy Bible, New Living Translation (NLT). Copyright ©2001 by Crossway Bibles, a publishing ministry of Good News Publishers. Contact me: openbibleinfo (at) gmail.com. Editor: Stephen Smith. Publication date: Oct 10, 2019. Publisher: OpenBible.info. Used by permission.

New Living Translation, copyright © 1996, 2004, 2015 by Tyndale House Foundation. Used by permission of Tyndale House Publishers, Inc., Carol Stream, Illinois 60188. All rights reserved.

Scripture quotations marked "ESV" are taken from the English Standard Version (ESV). The Holy Bible, English Standard Version. ESV® Text Edition: 2016. Copyright © 2001 by Crossway Bibles, a publishing ministry of Good News Publishers. Used by permission.

Transitions
ISBN: 978-1-7343918-0-0
Copyright © 2020 by Dr. Charles A. Kelly
Sounds of Sunrise, LLC

Printed in the United States of America. All rights reserved under International Copyright Law. Contents and/or cover may not be reproduced in whole or in part in any form without the express written consent of the Publisher or the Author.

Dedication

I dedicate this book to my wife Lisa of over 33 years. Thank you for being the love of my life and my best friend. Thank you for knowing what is best for me, even when I did not know what is best for myself. I love you, dearly. I also want to thank my children Charles J, Jason, Alexander, and Charlisa. Thank you for supporting me to accomplish writing this book. I hope that I have set an example of being committed to being faithful to God regardless of what comes our way in this life. I love all of you very much! I want to also thank my brother Carl. I am honored and blessed to have you as my twin. May God protect and bless you. Finally, I would like to dedicate this project to those people who feel like giving up and can't see their way out of a tough situation. God gives us the strength to endure and overcome.

We always think that life weighs us down, and this can be true in many cases. It is so important to understand that when you are talking about making it through situations and trials and tribulations, you cannot do this by yourself. There are so many times when we try to do things in our strength, and it is just not good enough. In many cases, we think that we are doing the right things, but we are outside of the will of God.

There are many times that the ills of the world can cause us to go into deep depressions but understand that Jesus came to overcome the world. He says this in his word, so be cheerful! To make it in life is really about Christ, to understand what His motives are, to understand what His plan is for your life, and to follow that plan so that He can bring the success in your life that you need. The only thing that can bring real success is having a relationship with Jesus Christ, understanding, and acting on his word.

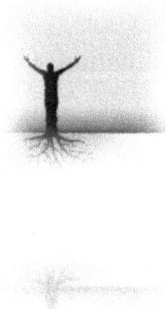

TABLE OF CONTENTS

PREFACE 7

CHAPTER 1 14
   Life's Challenges 14
      Job Loss 14
      Illness 33
      Death 39

CHAPTER 2 48
   Attacks 48
      Eighteen-Wheeler 48
      Bees 50
      Disease 52
      Stress and Anxiety 59

CHAPTER 3 69
   Being Tested 69
      Unexpected Setback 69
      Integrity 72
      Wait on God 74
      Gratitude 76
   Brokenness 82
      Divine sovereignty vs. human responsibility 82
      God's Will 84
      Rock Bottom 89
      Restoration 100

CHAPTER 4 107
   Standing on Faith 107
      Staying positive 107
      Putting on the Armor of God 110
      Determination and staying the course 115
   Grace 128
      He is enough 128
      Projects 130
      Breakthrough 135

CHAPTER 5 138
   Hope 138

  City contract *138*
  Encouragement *141*
 HEALING AND TRANSFORMATION 147
  Helping others *147*
  Musical Fulfillment *149*
  Educational Fulfillment *155*
  Employment Transition *158*
  Reconciliation and change *164*

CONCLUSION **171**

REFERENCES **174**

ABOUT THE AUTHOR **181**

Preface

The purpose of this book is to help anyone who is going through a period in life where they felt abandoned by God. The objective of this book is to give insight into seven years of my life's experience and explain it from multiple perspectives, with the guidance of scriptures from the bible. Feeling abandoned by God is a real issue for people, especially when they are dealing with things they have no control over. What can make matters worse is when there is no relief in sight. God knows what we go through. God also does not leave us alone. We need to know if we call *His* name and are one of *His* children, *His* grace '*is*' enough. God says, in his word, rely on Him for '*everything*.' He may not respond in our time, but he will come through in *His* time for *His* purpose. Romans 12:6 tells us, *"In his grace, God has given us different gifts for doing certain things well. So if God has given you the ability to prophesy, speak out with as much faith as God has given you."*

It is important to pray to God before bitterness or depression sets in. Just put your faith in Christ. God promises in his word that *He* will not give us more than we can bear. When we are tested by God and we *'pass,'* we are transformed for God's purpose. I pray this book can bring relief to people who are in need to learn from another person's experiences. Trust me; you are not alone when things go wrong. God will sustain everyone that comes to *Him* in *'faith'* and *'truth.'* 1 Corinthians 10:13 states the following, *"The temptations in your life are no different from what others experience. And God is faithful. He will not allow the temptation to be more than you can stand. When you are tempted, he will show you a way out so that you can endure."* Finally, we must remember what Psalm 27 tells us: *"The LORD is my light and my salvation— so why should I be afraid? The LORD is my fortress, protecting me from danger, so why should I tremble? When evil people come to devour me, when my enemies and foes attack me, they will stumble and fall. Though a mighty army surrounds me, my heart will not be afraid. Even if I am attacked, I will remain confident. The one thing I ask of the LORD — the thing I seek most— is to live in the house of the LORD all the days of my life, delighting in the LORD's perfections and meditating in his Temple. For he will conceal me there when troubles come; he will hide me in his sanctuary. He will place me out of reach on a high rock. Then I will hold my head high above my enemies who surround me. At his sanctuary, I will offer sacrifices with shouts of joy, singing, and praising the LORD with music. Hear me as I pray, O LORD. Be merciful and answer me! My heart has heard you say, "Come and talk with me." And my heart responds, " LORD, I am coming." Do not turn your back on me. Do not reject your servant in anger. You have always been my helper. Don't leave me now; don't abandon me, O God of my salvation! Even if my father and mother abandon me, the LORD will hold me close. Teach me how to live, O LORD. Lead me along the right path, for my enemies are waiting for me. Do not let me fall into their hands. For they accuse me of things I've never done; with every breath, they threaten me with violence. Yet I am confident I will see the LORD's goodness while I am here in the land of the living. Wait patiently for the LORD. Be brave and courageous. Yes, wait patiently for the LORD."*

*We must **believe** in God's plan for our lives to enjoy **real** transformation and purposeful living!*

Introduction

June 2013 started like any other time within this timeline in my life. I was traveling every week as a senior technical consultant working for SAP. I was working on a two-year project with EMC in Boston, several music projects, and my doctorate in business administration. Besides, I was the music director for a megachurch in Southern California. Family life was great, money was good, and I felt truly blessed to be alive. Although I was getting tired of traveling weekly for almost 20 years, I thought it was worth it because of the financial blessings, and having the ability to handsomely provide for my family, while creating projects to reach out and help others. I had a great transition plan for the next chapter of my life: become a professor, record and produce music and video projects, score films, and even write books. I had it all planned out, or so I thought. I didn't see what was about to happen, which turned out to be the beginning of the most challenging time in my life.

So many times, what we plan for our lives is different than what God intends for us. That's why it is critical to get on board with God's plan. Many times, we rebel against this and consequently delay or even short circuit our blessings. It is also many times more difficult to align with what God has in store for us because of the sacrifice, testing, and chastening. However, if we can endure the process, we will be blessed. In Romans 8:29, it says the following, *"For those whom he foreknew he also predestined to be conformed to the image of his Son, so that he might be the firstborn among many brothers (ESV)."* 1 Peter 4:12-13 states, *"Beloved, do not be surprised at the fiery trial when it comes upon you to test you, as though something strange was happening to you. But rejoice insofar as you share Christ's sufferings, that you may also rejoice and be glad when his glory is revealed (ESV)."* This is heavy stuff. It is not easy going through trials, tests, attacks, misery, and drama, but when we are a child of God, and He has us on the potter's wheel, we must recognize it for what it is if we are to live in the full blessing of God. Here is my testimony of a seven-year period in my life that was like none other. It was not comfortable, as I'm sure it wasn't for many others. However, when you are "*selected*" and you "*know*" you are selected, you must hold on to God's word. I hope my experience can assure you that you are "*not*" alone. Trust in Him, and He will help you to endure!

Chapter 1

Life's Challenges

Job Loss

Thursday, June 6th, 2013, started like any other day as a working SAP consultant. I left my hotel thinking about what I was going to take with me on the plane ride home. I was glad the week was coming to an end. I was excited about getting home to see my family. When I got to work, everything was normal. I was working on assignments, going to meetings, and engaging with colleagues.

Since my flight was in the late afternoon, I knew I needed to leave by 2 PM., so I planned accordingly. When 2 PM arrived, I signed out, told everyone I would see them the following week. As I was going back to the hotel, I got the phone call that would change my life. I got a call from an executive who worked for SAP. He told me to get to a place where he could talk to me. I told him I was driving, so let me pull into a place where I can speak. He began to tell me how sorry he was, but I didn't understand why he was sorry. He said, *"my name wasn't on the list,"* he didn't request it, and he didn't understand. I asked him what was going on. He then told me that I was getting laid off. At first, I was silent. Getting laid off was hard to digest since I was on a very profitable two-year project working with EMC. There were no complaints against me that I knew about, so I didn't understand the reason for being laid off. I immediately began to think about how I was going to tell my wife and family. Somewhat devastated but able to function, I drove to the hotel where I was staying and pulled into the parking lot.

I packed up and took all my belongings, checked out, and went to the airport. Even though this was devastating news, I told myself to be strong; God has always been with my family and me. He's gotten us through situations before, and he would get us through this one also. What I didn't realize is that God also puts people tests, and tests can become quite uncomfortable. The bible states in I Peter 1: 7, *"These trials will show that your faith is genuine. It is being tested as fire tests and purifies gold—though your faith is far more precious than mere gold. So, when your faith remains strong through many trials, it will bring you much praise and glory and honor on the day when Jesus Christ is revealed to the whole world."*

I realize this is not something we think about or even want to think about when we go through a difficult situation, such as losing a job, but God's word is real, and if we stay connected to the *Word*, God will not fail us.

When I got home, I told my wife, Lisa. She was very understanding and supportive. Having family support was a key component for me because I needed reinforcement, acceptance, and love in the worst way. The next day I began the job search process. I was confident finding a new job would not take long. After all, I had many years of work experience, an MBA, and wasn't fired because of something I did wrong. When reaching out to friends and associates, they were quick to respond. Based on the response, I felt it would take about a month to land another job. I continued working on my projects and enjoyed not having to travel weekly. I especially enjoyed being at home with my wife, children while I began to look at it as an extended vacation. After all, I still had paychecks coming in from SAP, a severance package, money saved up, stocks, and potential future work. After 20 years of traveling, this was perfect. We had a family reunion coming up, and my older son was graduating from college in Houston, Texas, which we all planned to attend. I felt one or two months of not working was well earned. However, I knew better not to waste time and become negligent in looking for work, so I continued looking. By the end of the month, I submitted my resume to over 100 openings and had a few interviews lined up. I said to myself, this will not take long.... However, it was the calm before the storm. In looking back, I now believe I made a mistake many of us make. Since things were lining up according to my prayers and God was blessing me, I thanked Him, *but* subconsciously I felt it was by my doing.

The Bible says this in Jeremiah 17:5-8 *"This is what the Lord says: "Cursed are those who put their trust in mere humans, who rely on human strength and turn their hearts away from the Lord. They are like stunted shrubs in the desert, with no hope for the future. They will live in the barren wilderness, in an uninhabited salty land. "But blessed are those who trust in the Lord and have made the Lord their hope and confidence. They are like trees planted along a riverbank, with roots that reach deep into the water. Such trees are not bothered by the heat or worried by long months of drought. Their leaves stay green, and they never stop producing fruit."* I trusted in God, but I also was too confident in myself. Many times, we feel we are the driving force behind successful endeavors. However, we cannot do anything lasting without relying on the confidence of God and being in *His* perfect will. I was about to learn this lesson.

After four months, I still was unemployed. Even when I went to Philadelphia for my mother's funeral in January 2014, I was vigorously looking for jobs, so I continued sending out resumes from my computer. I remember talking to a couple of recruiters that said they were sure I would get hired by the companies they represented. Although I was more focused on preparing for my mother's funeral, I still needed to take care of business because my family depended on me. Going into the fifth month of unemployment, I was praying and looking for February 2014 to give me a fresh start. During this time, the financial pressures were starting to wear on the family. In the beginning, Lisa and I were handling the stress ourselves, but now there was no hiding the struggles from the children. When there was little food to eat and shut off notices arriving in the mail, we felt it was better to have a family conversation about the situation. After all, our children were older and hopefully would understand. My primary concern was to get a job that will generate enough revenue to pay for the basic needs of the family. Since I was still unemployed, I decided to enroll for unemployment.

I felt a little guilty and embarrassed at first because I viewed it as taking free money. This was a prideful spirit because the truth was that I paid into the system for over 30 years, and this wasn't the time to be prideful. Besides, it would give me six months of income and buy additional time to find work. God tells us about the spirit of pride in Proverbs 29:23. The scripture says the following, *"Pride ends in humiliation, while humility brings honor,"* and James 4:6 says, *"God opposes the proud but gives grace to the humble."* Think about how many times we short circuit our blessings with prideful thinking? Therefore, it is *critical* to be covered with God's word, so it is part of our DNA.

After a few days went by, I separated myself from this spirit of pride and embraced the help, which was much needed and appreciated. This gave me a little more peace of mind while I continued to work on projects such as my doctorate degree and music productions while continuing to look for fulltime employment. This also gave time to heal from the death of my mother. There were times we needed money to pay bills and buy food. Without unemployment income, it would have been tough to make ends meet. I also had enough money to go to my doctoral residency in Phoenix, Arizona. I finally understood how much God was protecting us, and his grace is '*truly enough.*' We didn't go without our needs being met. During the next five months of receiving unemployment, God provided for our family many times, and it was much needed and appreciated. The month after the unemployment was over, I received a short contract that allowed me to make enough money to provide for the family.

God's grace in our lives is immeasurable. Hebrews 4:16 states, *"So let us come boldly to the throne of our gracious God. There we will receive his mercy, and we will find grace to help us when we need it most."* Romans 11:6 says, *"And since it is through God's kindness, then it is not by their good works. For, in that case, God's grace would not be what it really is—free and undeserved."* Finally, 2 Corinthians 12:9 states, *"Each time he said, "My grace is all you need. My power works best in weakness." So now I am glad to boast about my weaknesses so that the power of Christ can work through me."* We don't have to worry, become scared, or nervous if we come boldly to the throne of Christ and give our burdens to Him. This doesn't mean we should not do our part (we still have work to do); however, we *can't* do God's work for him. His piece will be done in *His* time, and we must believe his grace *is* enough. We must rest in this promise.

At the end of 2015, due to the loss of a contract, I went through another period of joblessness. We were still working through financial difficulties from the previous period of unemployment, and I was desperately looking for work again. I was also beginning to work on my taxes so we could get a refund. As Lisa and I continued explaining the situation to our children, they appeared to understand. However, what we didn't know how it would affect them as time went by. I later found out outside influences were a significant contribution to the stress being felt by being out of work. The combination of outside influences, inner conflicts, and circumstances beyond my control created an environment our family was not accustomed to. What made this even worse is that the more our children found out about the financial situation, the worse things got because it was in direct contrast to what they were accustomed to in the past. Looking back, I believe we shared with them information that they were not ready for. We had good intentions, but in hindsight, I think it was a mistake.

I was also praying, studying, and working closely with the church. I needed to get answers to why this was happening. I had no idea what I did that was so bad to bring all of this on myself and my family. I did, however, remember that God will test us to *"perfect"* us. I knew I had to hold onto this promise. Hebrews 13:5 states, *"Don't love money; be satisfied with what you have. For God has said, I will never fail you. I will never abandon you."* We become perfect in our weakness of our own capabilities and become *"strong"* when reliant on *"Him."* The question in this situation is, <u>what is the most effective way to successfully communicate being reliant on God to others when all they see is the negativity and urgency of the situation?</u> God responds in his word by saying, *"That's why I take pleasure in my weaknesses, and in the insults, hardships, persecutions, and troubles that I suffer for Christ. For when I am weak, then I am strong"* (2 Corinthians 12:10). This is a critical lesson to learn and *"required"* for *"true"* transformation to occur.

Multiple music production contracts kept the family going through the year 2016. This was a blessing from God, and

I knew He was providing for us. At the end of 2016, two of my sons landed jobs. I thought it was great they were interested in helping to pay family bills while creating a sense of independence for themselves. I love my children tremendously and was happy they were maturing. I wanted to do something special for them. Even though I wasn't making the kind of money I used to make, I was determined to buy each family member's Christmas gifts. It was obvious God was with us, and we needed to stay under His grace. It wasn't until May 2017 that I was offered a job as an adjunct professor at a community college. I knew this was a blessing, and God was pushing me into the direction He wanted me to go. However, the money was not adequate yet, so the struggle was real. My child that was struggling with the financial situation the most was becoming increasingly stressed out. This situation, along with previous issues, was making the communication and relationship difficult to handle. What made this especially hard was that at the time, I was didn't know why the relationship became so complicated. I found out later their struggle started much earlier than I knew about. Since I didn't have any idea what they were going through, I became more frustrated and concerned. In these situations, Proverbs 3:5-6 tells us, *"Trust in the Lord with all your heart; do not depend on your own understanding. Seek his will in all you do, and he will show you which path to take."* During the year 2018, while I was teaching college classes, I had to look for additional work because I needed to supplement my income. Even though Lisa and two of my sons were working, it still wasn't enough to carry the household. To make things more complicated, the college class I taught ended in July of 2018. My only financial contribution was the stipend I received from the church. The income was a great help, but it wasn't enough on its own. Again I was finding it hard to get work. This was very frustrating because I saw other people getting jobs without any problem. I kept asking God the same question, "why can't I find *steady* work?" The only thing I heard was, *"keep going."* It is a very frustrating experience when you have no control over a situation while being held to responsibilities you can't honor. Still, God was telling me to keep going and be patient. In Luke 12:22-26, the scriptures say, *"Then, turning to his disciples, Jesus said, "That is why I tell you not to worry about everyday life—whether you have enough food to eat or enough clothes to wear. For life is more than food, and your body more than clothing. Look at the ravens. They don't plant or harvest or store food in barns, for God feeds them. And you are far more valuable to him than any birds!*

Can all your worries add a single moment to your life? And if worry can't accomplish a little thing like that, what's the use of worrying over bigger things?"." Matthew 6:34 states the following, *"So don't worry about tomorrow, for tomorrow will bring its own worries. Today's trouble is enough for today."* Finally, Isaiah 55:8-11 states, *"My thoughts are nothing like your thoughts," says the Lord. "And my ways are far beyond anything you could imagine. For just as the heavens are higher than the earth, so my ways are higher than your ways and my thoughts higher than your thoughts. "The rain and snow come down from the heavens and stay on the ground to water the earth. They cause the grain to grow, producing seed for the farmer and bread for the hungry. It is the same with my word. I send it out, and it always produces fruit. It will accomplish all I want it to, and it will prosper everywhere I send it."* These scriptures are telling us NOT TO WORRY! God is in control, and *He will protect his own according to his will*. We must be diligent in prayer and trust God for everything else!

November 2018 was a pivotal month. I received an email that another college was hiring teachers from their job fair on the 16th of the month. I knew it was a long shot, but it was exactly what I needed to hear to give me hope. I set up my appointment and qualified for three interviews. The first interview was with the math and computer science department. The second was with the business group, and the third was with the music department. Since I've always wanted to teach music and I've been a musician all my life, this is what I was hoping for. It was a pleasant surprise that I got hired by the computer group. This was surprising in that I knew other people interviewed for the same position. I didn't do as well in the business interview. I believe this was because they were looking for someone who had more experience in the grading process and administrative skills. I had two years of teaching, but the classes didn't require a grade. This meant there were many things on the administrative end I didn't know about and needed to learn. However, I did get the breakthrough I was looking for. The music interview went very well, and they felt I was a good fit. I needed this breakthrough in the worse way, and I thanked God for blessing me with the opportunity. This didn't mean I had an assignment yet, but I would be allowed to get into their system just like my other community college. This made Thanksgiving special, with hope for an increase in revenue going forward. December 2018 left me anticipating teaching in the new year. When I started teaching new classes in January at my first college, I was hoping to teach classes at my new college as well. It would financially help tremendously if I taught two or three courses at the same time.

With all the tenseness, deep conversations, and praying for healing going on at home, knowing I would start teaching was just what I needed to hear, however, I was still going through slight depression. This was also the first year I didn't put up any Christmas decorations. I was really drained and felt it wasn't worth the effort. Some family members didn't care about the holidays, which drained me even more. Lisa and I, however, did honor our children who had birthdays in December. I was determined to get into a frame of mind to be productive going into the new year without the feeling of depression, anxiety, or stress. It became imperative to be surrounded by the Word, God's Spirit, and get back to having joy about being alive. Again, I didn't realize it then, but God was molding, growing, and healing my family and me all at the same time. It wasn't fun but *"necessary"* to be strong enough to carry out his purpose in our lives. His grace was, indeed, *"good enough."*

I started teaching a new class in January 2019. It felt good to be selected to teach a second class that was geared towards students working internships. Since this was a class I never taught, I didn't know what to expect. However, I was excited to learn how this class operated. Also, things at the church seemed to be going as usual, and I was still receiving and stipend; however, I could feel there was a significant change about to happen. Multiple people in the family were bringing in revenue, so that was a good thing. I appreciated the fact that numerous revenue streams kept us diversified.

During the Spring of 2019, I enjoyed teaching multiple classes. I also felt the students were excited about my enthusiasm and were being challenged positively. These students were some of the best in the entire program. I was teaching future scriptwriters, doctors, nurses, pastors, musicians, phycologists, photographers, and information technology talent. They interacted with each other perfectly. Even with the extra class work assigned, they were successfully meeting the challenge. Through the end of April 2019, classes continued to go well. The students were brilliant and worked very hard to maintain a high level of excellence. They were preparing presentations, term papers, resume, project career plans, cover letters, and job search strategies. This was being done on top of what they were doing in their other classes. In May 2019, my classes for the Spring semester ended. I was proud and pleased that my students passed with flying colors, and I knew they would do great things going forward.

During the end of the internship class, while meeting with student interns and their supervisors and managers, I received great news about each of them. I also got a chance to see a couple of my students give presentations to executive-level managers and they did great! Sometimes it was awkward scheduling meetings with each intern because they were scattered in many locations, but it was worth it.

Although it took a while, God transformed my life for his purpose. I could have done illegal things to make money, I could have performed unethical duties to ease the burden and pain. However hard it was and scary it became, <u>*I remained faithful to God and the Word.*</u> He will transform your life also if you stay committed to *Him*. He is not a respecter of persons. Acts 10:34 states, *"Then Peter replied, "I see very clearly that God shows no favoritism."* Romans 2:11 says, *"For God does not show favoritism."* Finally, in Ephesians 6:8-9, the scriptures say, *"Remember that the Lord will reward each one of us for the good we do, whether we are slaves or free. Masters treat your slaves in the same way. Don't threaten them; remember, you both have the same Master in heaven, and he has no favorites."* His word will not come back void. If he did it for me, He would do it for you. Just understand through all the trials and challenges, stay *faithful and trust in the Lord*. It's your *"key"* to overcoming tests, challenges attacks, and in this case, job loss.

Illness

When I arrived in Philadelphia on January 1st, 2014, for my mother's funeral, I was in disarray. So many things were falling apart, and I didn't know why. However, the one thing I knew I had to do was be strong, not just for myself but for my family. When I arrived in Philadelphia, I didn't talk to people about my personal issues even though I was trying not to be consumed by the jobless situation. In looking back, I don't know if this was a good decision because I needed an outlet from the negativity. Unhealthy thoughts can become threatening to a person's peace of mind. I did, however, discuss certain things with Lisa, hopefully without becoming a burden. She was holding down everything at home, and the last thing I wanted to do was bring my inner thoughts into our home, which was our *"safe haven."* Lisa was very supportive, and I really loved her for that. For example, I remember telling her how disappointed I was with the condition of the Philadelphia neighborhood I grew up in. I began to discuss a situation that happened while going to the library to get internet access. I ran into a person that knew me when I was a teenager. He said we grew up and attended high school together. I really didn't recognize him at first. He looked much older than me and was missing many teeth. The gentleman said he remembered watching me perform at music concerts when I was in local Philadelphia bands. He indicated how great those events were. At first, I didn't remember many of the events being discussed, but I began to remember. He was very detailed and descriptive. This conversation went on for about 20 minutes, and then I finally recognized who he was, and tears came to my eyes. I gave him a big hug and said, "*now I remember you!*" He smiled, and we both laughed. Since this was a great bonding moment, I felt comfortable in asking how he was really doing and what has transpired in his life. He told me he had cancer and didn't have too much longer to live. He also said he was grateful for the moments we shared as friends, and he immediately asked me about myself. While I talked to him, I began to feel guilty. I said to myself, "this man is dying, and God is *still* fighting my battles, so I have no reason to complain." My health was good, and *God's grace is enough.* I then understood the importance of thanking God, prayer, and staying under his anointment, regardless of the circumstances and difficulties of life. I thanked him for our conversation, we exchanged numbers, and he left. I said to myself, here is a man with cancer looking 30 years older than he was. *Yet* he was *happy*. If he could do it, so could I. This gave me a sense of inspiration, strength, and purpose. I finished my business at the library and left, but with a different perspective.

Psalm 41:3 states, *"The Lord nurses them when they are sick and restores them to health."* Romans 5:1-5 says,

"Therefore, since we have been made right in God's sight by faith, we have peace with God because of what Jesus Christ our Lord has done for us. Because of our faith, Christ has brought us into this place of undeserved privilege where we now stand, and we confidently and joyfully look forward to sharing God's glory. We can rejoice, too, when we run into problems and trials, for we know that they help us develop endurance. And endurance develops strength of character, and character strengthens our confident hope of salvation. And this hope will not lead to disappointment. For we know how dearly God loves us because he has given us the Holy Spirit to fill our hearts with his love." Finally, Jeremiah 30:17-24 says, *"I will give you back your health and heal your wounds," says the Lord. "For you are called an outcast 'Jerusalem[a] for whom no one cares.'" This is what the Lord says: "When I bring Israel home again from captivity and restore their fortunes, Jerusalem will be rebuilt on its ruins, and the palace reconstructed as before. There will be joy and songs of thanksgiving, and I will multiply my people, not diminish them; I will honor them, not despise them. Their children will prosper as they did long ago. I will*

establish them as a nation before me, and I will punish anyone who hurts them. They will have their own ruler again, and he will come from their own people. I will invite him to approach me," says the Lord, "for who would dare to come unless invited? You will be my people, and I will be your God." Look! The Lord's anger bursts out like a storm, a driving wind that swirls down on the heads of the wicked. The fierce anger of the Lord will not diminish until it has finished all he has planned. In the days to come, you will understand all this." I believe my friend found joy, knowing God would protect him. How many times are we making an illness worse by what we say, how we act, and believing things we shouldn't. In times of illness, we must *speak life* to our lives and *reject negativity*. The enemy wants us to be stressed, filled with negativity and anxiety instead of standing on God's Word. Regardless of the doctor's report, God will have the last say. We must stay in prayer and do things that are in alignment with God's purpose. To understand what His goal is, we *must* read His word.

My friend knew the power of his words and his mindset. He made sure he didn't speak negatively. Despite facing life-threatening sickness, he stayed positive, and you must remain positive also. Don't make it easy for the enemy to infiltrate your thoughts. Exodus 15:26 states, *"He said, "If you will listen carefully to the voice of the Lord your God and do what is right in his sight, obeying his commands and keeping all His decrees, then I will not make you suffer any of the diseases I sent on the Egyptians; for I am the Lord who heals you."* This is important because true healing comes from the Lord. Doctors have their role and are very instrumental to the healing process, but if we are aligned with Christ, *miracles can happen.*

Illness is part of life. Eventually, each of us will either know someone or will face some form of disease ourselves in the future. We must understand that Christ will fight this battle for us on our behalf *if* we allow him. James 5:14-15 states, *"Are any of you sick? You should call for the elders of the church to come and pray over you, anointing you with oil in the name of the Lord. Such a prayer offered in faith will heal the sick, and the Lord will make you well. And if you have committed any sins, you will be forgiven."*

Death

December 2013 started out with bad news. I was informed my childhood friend, and fellow musician Linwood Grey passed away from leukemia. This hurt quite a bit. I knew Linwood since I was six years old. We grew up together on the same block, and we both were involved in the Philadelphia music scene. I wanted to go back and attend his funeral but unfortunately didn't have the money. During this time, I was also starting to feel the financial weight of being unemployed, now dealing with close friends dying, was a bit depressing. Even though people close to me were dying, I had to keep sending out resumes. However, I was not getting much response because the IT industry had shut down for the holidays. Regardless of the obstacles, I had to keep looking. I was also swamped working on the music production for the Christmas season services at church. Besides, I was planning to go to Phoenix, Arizona, during the month in February 2014 for my doctoral residency. While all these responsibilities and notifications of people close to me dying, the one thing that weighed on me the most was the health of my mother. She was suffering from dementia. During my last conversation with my mother, I was having a challenging time listening to her on the phone, without getting emotional and crying. I remember talking to her on Christmas Day, and hearing her tell me how much she loved me, and that I was her *"heart."* I also told her I loved her very much. During this conversation, it appeared she was getting better, and I was encouraged.

However, I will never forget the phone call I received on Saturday, December 28th, 2013, from my brother. He told me our mother passed away. This was crushing. I loved my mother dearly, and this was the call I dreaded. It finally hit me that both of my parents were deceased. Knowing both parents are diseased breeds an empty feeling of loss and finality. What made this even harder is that the next morning, I had to play at church and lead worship. Looking back, I never had time to digest my circumstances. I remembered while playing at church, tears rolled down my face while making sure everyone else on the worship team had what they needed to lead the congregation into a worshipful experience. My brother witnessed both of our parents pass away, and he really needed help. He also was not in the best of health. Even though I didn't have much money to get a plane ticket, I had to get to Philadelphia. What made matters worse was this was the holiday season, and my family needed me home in California. It was during this time I started to understand God's grace is enough. He was the *only* one who could get me through this period of my life. I had to turn to *Him*, and I did. God provided a way for me to go back to Philadelphia on Tuesday, December 31st. This was the most challenging plane trip of my life.

When I arrived at my mother's house, I knew there was a lot of work to do. Because my brother took care of my mother, the house desperately needed cleaning. There was a problem with this, however. My brother owned a dog and a cat. He was very fond of them, but the dog and I didn't get along well. My brother's dog would jump on me as a way of bonding. Looking back at this now, I should have responded differently and been friendlier. The dog and I had different perspectives of the house. My brother's dog thought the house belonged to her, and *I was a visitor*. I looked at it as this was my mother, father, and brother's home. *She* was a visitor. For example, when I would try to clean up, she would give me resistance, growl, and bark. This led to a certain level of concern. I finally decided to just clean my parent's room. However, when I saw its condition, I began to emotionally break down. My parents prided themselves on keeping an immaculate house. It took me three days to get it clean enough where I felt comfortable. While I was working in the room, I relived many memories, and all of them good. My parents were married for 54 years before my father passed away in 1999. We were a stable family. During this time of cleaning, I started to make the room into a shrine for my parents. I set up each side of the bed just how they kept it when I left home in 1983. I know how this might sound strange to some people, but I felt this was necessary for them and myself. I couldn't leave their room in poor condition, and I felt this was the least I could do. I began to collect historical items such as pictures, magazines, jewelry, portraits, letters, documents, and anything else I could find that told my life's story. I felt I was looking into a window of the past. This was intimate, therapeutic, painful, and *much needed*. It also helped to put together those forgotten pieces of my life and move forward. This gave me the courage to dig deep into the past and realize how precious life is, and without putting God first, I was reminded we cannot live under anointment and blessing.

After I cleaned up, I immediately began preparing for the funeral service, and the weather was not cooperating. I can remember during New Year's weekend, Philadelphia received a couple of feet of snow, and everyone was snowed in. I went to the store to load up on groceries. When I came back, I stayed in my parent's bedroom and worked on my mother's obituary. I was proud of the fact that my parents met at Tuskegee Airforce Base during WWII, got married, and never separated. Also, my father was an airplane mechanic working with the Tuskegee Airmen. My mother worked on the airplanes as well. They often would tell me to *"know who you are"* and *"never let someone else define you."* Knowing what my parents told me, along with God's Spirit and scripture helped me to stay focused and sharp. I started to think about how to help pay for my mother's funeral and send for my family to come out to Philadelphia. Since money was now an issue, I had to rely on God to provide. I believe since I was in constant prayer and standing on His word, I was able to get money from old stocks, I totally forgot about. Two of Lisa's sisters helped also. This was truly unexpected and really needed. My mother did have life insurance and funeral arrangements, but the amount was not enough due to the age of the policy date. Although I knew God was providing for us, this was the first of many instances during this period of life, which I call the *"Job Test."* (The *"Job Test"* is based on Job in the bible. The bible states that Job was financially successful and blessed with a loving wife, three daughters, and seven sons. Job lived in an area called Uz with his immediate and extended family. Job owned seven thousand sheep, three thousand camels, five hundred yokes of oxen, five hundred donkeys, and had a large number of servants. Scripture (Job 1:1) also states Job was *"blameless and upright; he feared God and shunned evil."* God removed the hedge around Job to show Satan that Job will not curse God because he truly loved Him. When the hedge is removed, Job goes through a series of tests, trials, and tribulations. Although God prohibited Satan from taking Job's life, Satan was allowed by God to inflict terrible suffering on Job as a *"test"* to Job's loyalty to God. This is the basis of the *"Job Test."*) Although it was hardly ever in my timing, God always came through for me when I needed him the most.

    When my family arrived in Philadelphia, I could not let them stay in the house, so I needed to get a hotel. Although money again was an issue, I had reward points. I did not realize I had enough for four children and two adults, but yet we were taken care of. It must be understood how hard this was for me not to be in control of anything and to be forced to only rely on

God. For over twenty years, I made over six figures annually. Now I was unemployed, relying strictly on Him.

On the day of the funeral, it was snowing, wet, and cold. I appreciated people coming out to pay my mother last respects. While most of her friends were dead, My Aunt Maurice was alive and well. It was great to see her and my cousins from Dallas, Texas, and Georgia. Although my family was spread out in different locations throughout the country, we were still close, and talking to them again was refreshing. After the burial, the entire family spent time together at the repast. God came through once again to provide the money from unexpected sources. It turned out I had just enough Marriot rewards to cover the expenses. This was the second time during this *"Job Test"* period God provided. Again, I didn't know His purpose, but I did know He was in control. Proverbs 19:21 says, *"You can make many plans, but the Lord's purpose will prevail."* This can be frustrating. However, it's a valuable lesson. The bottom line is that we must be in *alignment* with God's purpose. Therefore, we must find out what that is.

When we arrived home back in California, I was still mourning the death of my mother. I would take hours looking at the archives I brought back with me from Philadelphia. I spent days putting together pieces of my life and my parent's lives that I didn't know existed. Although I appreciated going through this phase, I began to realize I was starting to become depressed. Depression is a silent killer, and I didn't have time for it. Since I was unemployed, I couldn't afford to spend time being concerned about my loss. Maybe under normal circumstances, this would be permissible, but I had to find a job. In looking back, I realize the importance of taking enough time to mourn the loss of loved ones but not to the point of falling into depression. Matthew 5:4 says, *"God blesses those who mourn, for they will be comforted."* However, in Revelation 21:4, the scriptures say, *"He will wipe every tear from their eyes, and there will be no more death or sorrow or crying or pain. All these things are gone forever."* We must allow the Holy Spirit to heal us from loss of life. It can take time, and it's critical to be sensitive to what the Spirit tells us to do.

Chapter 2

Attacks

Eighteen-Wheeler

June 2014 was the first month where attacks started to really pick up. After my second son, Jason's graduation, my oldest son, CJ, was in town for the ceremony. It was great for all of us to be together! Talking with CJ, he wanted to return the car I purchased for him because he bought a new vehicle. This was fine with me because we needed another car to get around. After graduation, I flew to Dallas, Texas, where the car was, so I could drive it back home to California. It was also nice to see where my son was living. He was working as an accountant with BNSF. I was thrilled he was doing well and loved him dearly. After spending a couple of days with my son, I began the journey back to California. If you've ever driven through Texas, you know it takes 10-12 hours to get from the eastern part of the state to the western part. Since I've taken this drive before, I was prepared. About three to four hours into the trip, I noticed there was an eighteen-wheeler diesel truck approaching me very quickly on the passenger side. I was in the farthest lane on the left, next to a wall. Vehicles were in front of me and on the passenger side next to me. I was boxed in. The truck was moving so fast the other vehicles were being forced to drive faster. As this truck pulled next to me, it started to enter my lane. This was very scary because I literally had nowhere to go. The driver started to cut me off. The only recourse I had was to slow down a little, so he could enter my lane without hitting me. As I began to slow down, he cut in front of me and sideswiped my car, tearing off the mirror and damaging the passenger side. Due to the impact, I hit the wall on the driver's side. I was terrified because this was a life and death situation. As it turned out, the wall prevented the truck from flipping my car. I would have also been pinned to the wall if I didn't slow down. What made matters worse is that this truck was full of pigs and cows. The sheer weight of this type of vehicle would have crushed me. When the driver of the eighteen-wheeler cut in front of me, he also didn't stop. He kept going, making the situation a hit and run. When I saw he wasn't going to stop, I called my insurance company and 911. The police located where we were, and they followed him. I wasn't going to let this guy get him away with hitting me. While I was on the phone with the officers, I gave them the description of the truck and his license plate. I also took pictures of the vehicle. The police finally stopped him and determined he was drunk. They gave me his insurance information, and I was able to continue my trip. Even though I suffered passenger damage to the body of the car, and the mirror was completely gone, I was thankful to God for sparing my life. I was also able to get home safely, and I got the car fixed. Again, God's grace was good enough. This was the *first* test.

Bees

About a week after getting home from Dallas, I was working from my house when the next test occurred. I was in my studio when I looked out the window. I saw about fifteen or twenty bees swarming. Since I've been through this before, I was concerned. I was also allergic to bees. When I was a child, I almost died of bee stings. When I went outside, what I saw was shocking. There were thousands of bees swarming outside in front of the window to my studio. I immediately called a company that specializes in bee removal. They came out and told me it was likely bees in the wall. I was nervous because I could not only hear them from my studio, there were bees in the bathroom next to my studio room. I told the workers to do what you needed to do to eliminate them. They first removed the threat of bees that were flying around. Secondly, they checked to see if bees entered the wall of the attic. What they found was startling. Not only did they get into the wall, but they created a beehive full of honey about five feet long. I had no choice but to have the workers remove the hive. From what I was told, the cost in most situations like mine was in the thousands of dollars. This is where God showed up again. As it turned out, the bees found a hollow wall, so the repair cost was minimal. The workers were able to remove all the honey. They also sprayed chemicals to prevent the pheromones from attracting more bees. I knew I was deep into God's *"Job Test,"* and every time he came through. This was the *second* test.

 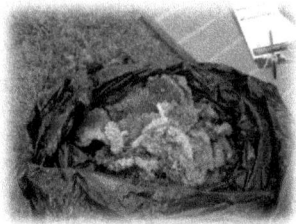

Disease

In July 2014, my son Jason graduated from high school and was awarded a partial scholarship to go to CBU. Lisa and I were very pleased with this because he really worked hard. Jason is a wonderful young man. We love him dearly and wanted only the best for him. It was early June when Lisa and I went to the campus to check out where Jason would go to school. We thought it would be a great idea for him to live on campus. This would allow him to live on his own while being in a Christian environment. I was very pleased with the living conditions and felt he would grow into adulthood successfully.

A couple of weeks later, we came back to CBU to get him registered for the fall. Even though it was a hot day, Jason was unusually thirsty. He then started to complain about not feeling well. Since it was uncharacteristic of him to feel sick, we quickly finished the registration process, bought him water and food, and quickly went home so he could rest. This was interesting because my other son Alexander (aka Alex), had contracted a strange disease that broke out into a rash that looked like hives. It was also very itchy. It was so bad I made the decision to take him to the hospital because the rash was getting worse. I had to take Jason with me even though he was not feeling well.

    When we got to the hospital, the emergency doctors immediately attended to Alex because the breakout was getting worse. They admitted him, and he was taken to the emergency room. During this exact moment, Jason passed out. Witnessing something like this was extremely unnerving, and I tried not to panic. I had to have *both of my sons admitted at the same time at the same hospital*. I called Lisa so she could come to the hospital. I then went to attend to both sons. I found myself running from one room to another. While checking on Alex, I saw his entire body was covered with an itchy rash. I was very concerned, but the doctors said he would be ok within a few days. That gave me a better feeling. However, when I went back to Jason's room, he passed out again. I clearly remember him saying, "*Dad?*" and then his vital signs dropped. With tears in my eyes, I called out to the nurses and doctors. They rushed back to attend to him, and they were nervous. I began praying and asking God to please save my son. The doctors continued to work on him, but by now, he was unconscious. After ten minutes, his vital signs started to rise, and he opened his eyes. He also was covered with the same rash Alex had. Finally, the doctors confirmed they both contracted Hand-Foot-and-Mouth Disease.

    This viral infection is very contagious. It is usually contracted by young children. However, both Alex and Jason were young adults. The symptoms characterized by Hand-Foot and Mouth Disease are sores in the mouth and a rash on the hands and feet. This disease is most commonly caused by a coxsackievirus, and there is no specific treatment. How they got this, I don't know for sure, but discussing the situation with Alex, he told me he drank water from an outside public water fountain. Since this disease is very contagious, it is safe to assume Alex transferred it to Jason because they were together playing basketball. The doctors said the reason Jason passed out three times was due to dehydration. The doctors and nurses gave him a few quarts of liquids intravenously.

I know God has a purpose for everything, but this was hard for me or any parent to see their child pass out three times while in the hospital. Satan was trying hard, but again we were protected by God's grace. I believe this was the *third* test. God let us know he was in control. Ephesians 6:12 lets us know attacks start in the spiritual world. It says, *"For we are not fighting against flesh-and-blood enemies, but against evil rulers and authorities of the unseen world, against mighty powers in this dark world, and against evil spirits in the heavenly places."* It is critical to understand this and not react to just the physical assault. People cannot win this type of fight without the power of the Word. We must be in constant prayer and stay faithful. At times it can be challenging; however, being faithful to God is the key to protecting ourselves against the attacks of the enemy. Psalm 91 states the following: *"Those who live in the shelter of the Most High will find rest in the shadow of the Almighty. This I declare about the Lord: He alone is my refuge, my place of safety; he is my God, and I trust him. For he will rescue you from every trap and protect you from deadly disease. He will cover you with his feathers. He will shelter you with his wings. His faithful promises are your armor and protection. Do not be afraid of the terrors of the night, nor the arrow that flies in the day. Do not dread the disease that stalks in darkness, nor the disaster that strikes at midday. Though a thousand fall at your side, though ten thousand are dying around you, these evils will not touch you. Just open your eyes and see how the wicked are punished. If you make the Lord your refuge, if you make the Most High your shelter, no evil will conquer you; no plague will come near your home. For he will order his angels to protect you wherever you go. They will hold you up with their hands, so you won't even hurt your foot on a stone. You will trample upon lions and cobras; you will crush fierce lions and serpents under your feet! The Lord says, "I will rescue those who love me. I will protect those who trust in my name. When they call on me, I will answer; I will be with them in trouble. I will rescue and honor them. I will reward them with a long life and give them my salvation."*

Both sons spent the night in the hospital and came home the next day. It took about three weeks for them to heal. Although the itching and nastiness of the rash were gone, there were still brown scars that eventually healed over time.

When I thought we were over this horrible situation, I noticed a rash forming on my body. At first, I was not too concerned, but when the itching started, I knew I also contracted Hand-Foot-and-Mouth Disease. After three hours, the disease overtook my body, and I needed to be quarantined. I was isolated to our bedroom and needed to run the air conditioner 24 hours a day. Also, I had a fever and was experiencing dizziness. Being a man in his fifties, it was more difficult for the body to fight the virus than if a younger person contracted the disease. It took quite a bit longer for me to recover than it took my sons. I remember lying on my back and telling myself, *"what did I do to deserve this?"*

After the second week, I had to get out of bed because of job interview commitments. I felt better, but the rash was still showing a little. The bigger and older bumps were turning brown. I was concerned this would be detrimental to the interview process, but I had no choice. Fortunately, some interviews were remote. However, the one I needed to personally attend was with PWC. I knew the brown marks were showing, and I wasn't one hundred percent, but this was with the hiring manager.

When I met him, I could tell he could see the marks on my neck and hands. I had to rise above it as much as I could. Even though he saw scares on my hands, he didn't mention anything to me. I was also concerned because I didn't want to spread it to anyone I encountered. After the interview, I went home and rested. I was hoping I did well, but either way, I was happy I got through it. Although I found out later, I didn't get the job (and didn't know why), it was good to know God is still protecting me. This could have been a lot worse. Ephesians 6:11 says, *"Put on all of God's armor so that you will be able to stand firm against all strategies of the devil"* and James 1:2-4 says *"Dear brothers and sisters when troubles of any kind come your way, consider it an opportunity for great joy. For you know that when your faith is tested, your endurance has a chance to grow. So, let it grow, for when your endurance is fully developed, you will be perfect and complete, needing nothing."* Again, God's grace is enough. This was the *fourth* test.

Stress and Anxiety

February 2015 saw me pulled into a struggle at my job and business. I guess you can call it a political war. This was an election season, and there were a few things to be concerned about. The Mayor and Mayor Pro-Tem were running against each other. Rumors were flying around that by helping the Mayor with a concert, I would help her win the election. I wasn't thinking like this at all. I wanted to contribute to bringing the first jazz festival to the city and its citizens. While I wasn't involved in the planning, I was the connection to artists, production people, and business personnel that could produce a successful event. Basically, I was guilty by association. Mayor Pro-Tem wanted desperately to win the election and was determined to do whatever was necessary. This group of people even opened an investigation that went up to Sacramento Ca. It was quickly determined there was no wrongdoing. However, this didn't make my political issue better or go away. Mayor Pro-Tem and his group seemed determined to do whatever was necessary to stop the concert from happening. It was said they were going to *"takedown"* whoever was involved. Even though I was warned and concerned, I couldn't let this stop me from my real job. I became more associated with the concert than the job I was going for the city. I was starting to find out how nasty, mean, and hostile politics can be. The other dilemma was that I am a Christian. I quickly found out some political groups do not want to be associated with religion. Not that I was trying to do this, but it is who I am. The question that soon became apparent was should I "*stand down*" and back out the concert. This was a real dilemma because I connected many people to the show, and my family was telling me not to cave in. I felt I would look weak in their eyes if I excluded my participation.

On the other hand, if I kept going, I would run the risk of being politically assassinated. This was a hard decision. After much prayer, I decided to continue. My family said they would back me if there were any consequences from my decision. This would be easier said than done.

Things were going well in March 2015 at work, other than the political issues, which created a tense environment at work. Mayor Pro-Tem was still upset about the Mayor's concert, and he was trying to do everything he could to stop it. To make matters worse, the person in charge of overseeing the administrative process was making plenty of mistakes. It started to make me second guess my decision to help the Mayor. During the SoundsOfSunrise vocal rehearsal, I discussed some of these issues with the team. However, I also told them it was critical to bring God's word to the masses. It was vital for them to be aware of certain things so they could pray and not get consumed by negativity.

April 2015 arrived, and there were still lots to do for the jazz festival, such as selling a significant number of tickets for the Mayor's concert. Most ticket concerns were linked to the inability of the city council to get behind the festival due to political concerns. This was a tragedy because the event could have been something that brought the city together. To have politicians turn something meant for good into something divisive was unfortunate and a real eye-opener. While I felt this could jeopardize my contract with the city due to my connection to the event, I was still committed to supporting the concert. I asked many people, including family members, friends, and associates, should I stay or pull out? Most people said it was better to continue being involved with the event rather than stand down. After all, if I gave in, it still might not change my opposition's position regarding my contract. It would have been a double hit to pull out of the event *and* lose my deal. I decided to continue and support the concert.

When the day of the festival arrived, it was cold and rainy. This was one of the mistakes made in planning. Typically, April in this part of the country, the weather is unpredictable in terms of temperature and precipitation. Although the average percentage of a chance of rain is between five and ten percent. The average temperature range for the 25th of April 52 to 76 degrees. On April 25th, 2015, the temperature range was 53 to 60 degrees, the wind blue gusts up to 25 mph, and it was rainy and damp. There were only four months to plan, and most people felt it wasn't enough time to do it correctly. Typically, the month of April has always been a little early in the outdoor season, weather-wise.

In the morning, we prepared for the rain as much as we could. It was critical to protect musicians, singers, and equipment. The artists who participated were great. Everyone performed well, and the people who came were happy. Because of the rain, and low temperature, the crowd was small; however, it was considered a success. After the concert was over, my concern shifted to the political fallout. God's word says many things about dealing with stress and anxiety. Philippians 4:6-7 says, *"Don't worry about anything; instead, pray about everything. Tell God what you need and thank him for all he has done. Then you will experience God's peace, which exceeds anything we can understand. His peace will guard your hearts and minds as you live in Christ Jesus."* We must understand faith is the opposite of fear. It is critical to let God fight our battles. John 14:27 says, "I am leaving you with a gift—peace of mind and heart. And the peace I give is a gift the world cannot give. So, don't be troubled or afraid."

August 2015 was a pivotal month. The City determined it would hire Information Technology employees and allow contracts from consultants to expire. This was a business model change. For many years they didn't have IT personnel, and to do so now I felt was directly related to politics. From a business perspective, it did make sense, but with the shift happening so quickly, it had me concerned. I was told if I applied for one of the positions, there would be a good chance I could be hired. From what I understood, the City preferred to hire people they were familiar with, and this would have been the perfect scenario for me. However, with the political controversy, this could be used to eliminate my position. I realized I didn't have control over any decisions. All I could do was produce stellar work, create a transformational environment, and help the City to achieve its objectives. I decided to apply for a position.

I went on the interviews and was expected to get hired. However, I was told by someone that I should have gotten hired, but with the current political climate, they didn't want to cause additional problems; therefore, it was better to hire the other person I was competing with. This was another blow, and I was back to where I started from an employment perspective. By the beginning of October, my contract expired, and my time at the City was over. At this point, I wanted to make a point to be as professional as possible. I made sure all projects were completed, and I stayed positive. People at the City who knew the truth were upset because, during this period, information technology work was really getting done. There was history within the City that politics many times prevented progress from occurring, and this was the main reason why good people would leave. However, I couldn't allow myself to be concerned about that. My objective was to find work. I was finally caught up with my bills, and the last thing I needed was to fall behind again, so I started to send out resumes and talk to recruiters. Even though I was mentally dealing with the loss of a contract, I couldn't forget to work on my doctorate degree as well. I was starting my fourth year, and I was too far into the process, not to succeed. Mentally this was tough to handle, but I remembered God's word, which says in 2 Timothy 1:7 *"for God has not given us a spirit of fear, but of power and of love and of a sound mind."* I had to stand on that. Besides, the main reason I needed to succeed was to show my children they could get their education and succeed in life. My family was my priority, and I had to make sure they were ok. I had to keep revenue coming in because, for more than twenty years, I was the provider, and everyone depended on that. I knew they would support me, but I didn't know how long it would take to get the next contract or job. Regardless of the issues, God gave us grace and protected us. However, the following tests and most severe attacks were not too far away.

October 2015 was a month I have since questioned my decisions. My family was working on multiple projects. Since I wasn't working with the City, the cash flow wasn't there to finance the project. I only had enough money to sustain the family through November. So, I had to do something quickly. This is where I now can look back and see I lost my faith in God and made decisions on my own, which turned out to be detrimental. As I was going through the self-analysis process, I really should have thought through my choices much better. I was afraid of losing the financial momentum I gained over the past year. I, therefore, told myself I needed to do whatever it took to maintain cash flow. This is where I should have *listened* to the Holy Spirit, but I fell short.

I was starting to become concerned about how these changes and situations were affecting my children. One child was coming back home from living on campus at college. We didn't have the money to pay for college going into the next semester. This bothered me a great deal because he deserved to go to college. Another child just graduated from high school, and I wanted him to go to college also. Even though he was on the fence about going in the fall, I wanted to still give him a choice. What concerned me, in particular, was that one of my children felt we didn't care about them because there were things we weren't in the position at that time to give them. The lesson I learned during this period is that <u>God provides the things we need and the things He wants us to have, but that doesn't mean he gives us everything we want.</u> Matthew 6:31-32 says, *"So don't worry about these things, saying, 'What will we eat? What will we drink? What will we wear?' These things dominate the thoughts of unbelievers, but your heavenly Father already knows all your needs."* We are not in control, *God is*. This is a hard lesson to learn, but if we want *real* success, it is critical to get these scriptures into our spirit. Attacks can be hard handle; however, we must use scripture to counteract them. I have learned to live by Romans 12:12, which states, "Rejoice in our confident hope. Be patient in trouble, and keep on praying."

Chapter 3

Being Tested

Unexpected Setback

Chico's is located in Fort Myers. It was a fun organization to work for! I was doing exciting work, so the stress wasn't didn't bother me. The team I worked with appeared to be a great group of people, the hotel wasn't far from the job location, and the weather was great in Florida. I was told the contract was going to be for many months with the possibility of an extension. This made me happy because I could then plan to finance additional projects, save money, and continue to support the family the way they were accustomed to. Approximately two months into the project, I received a phone call. I was informed the contract was over. I was stunned. Again, I didn't see it coming, and neither did the people I was working with. I was really shaken because this put me back into searching for another job, and I was not emotionally ready for that. Since my family depended on me to provide for them, I didn't have the luxury to think about what happened I had to start looking for work quickly. Looking back at this period, I was subconsciously beginning to question why God was doing this and did I do something wrong. I didn't realize it then, but I now know I was in the first quarter of my *"Job Test."*

I knew unemployment during the Fall season had to be taken seriously. The information technology industry shuts down for the holidays, and I knew it could take me a while to find something. Understanding this, I sent out hundreds of resumes to potential jobs searching for opportunities. I had to stay focused because of my responsibility to other people. I was helping my brother through a complicated situation, I was the music director at my church, and this was one of the busiest times of the year. I was also working on my doctorate while very much into the details, producing the "I Believe" music project. Since the holiday season was approaching, I knew it was important I stayed positive and not let the pressure show. Again, many people depended on me, most importantly, my family. However, I was entering the eye of the storm, and another "*Job Test*" was beginning.

I felt mentally healthy enough and was relying on God to work things out, so I continued sending out resumes and applying for jobs. After a while, I had a phone interview with an energy company in Houston, Texas, which went very well. So well, in fact, they offered me a three to four-month contract. I said to myself this was great because I really needed the money. As I prepared to drive from California to Houston, I was aware of the pitfalls of the drive. Many times, police will stop people with out of state license plates and question where they are going. I made sure to take things with me to prove I was coming to Houston for work. This meant I printed out my onboarding documents, itinerary, the hotel was staying in, and other vial things. Being an African American male traveling this route by myself can be challenging, so it was critical to be prepared for everything. As I thought I might be, I was stopped in Arizona and Texas. I believe they wanted to see if I was carrying drugs, weapons, or something illegal. I'm a Christian man rooted in the word of God, so drugs and guns or other illicit things don't enter my mind. However, police officers don't know this, and you never know their real purpose or objectives. When they talked to me, I was calm, pleasant, and compliant. I gave them no reason to escalate the situation. There are many more profound subjects I could discuss here, but I will only leave you with this comment: I let the Holy Spirit guide me and speak through me. This was another test. John 16:13 says, *"When the Spirit of truth comes, he will guide you into all truth. He will not speak on his own but will tell you what he has heard. He will tell you about the future."*

Integrity

Later that month, I arrived in Houston on a Sunday afternoon and needed to be at work the next day. I was tired and needed to rest, so I checked into the hotel, took a shower, ate, and went to sleep. I arrived at work and thought this was going to be great. My son was in Houston, and I felt this would be a time to bond with him. The first meeting on the job was interesting. The people appeared to be helpful, but I began to see I was put into an awkward situation. There were two different groups with different opinions on how to handle specific processes. It became apparent to me I was brought in to support the people who hired me *even* if they were in the *wrong*. This was a dilemma because I needed the money and didn't want to lose the contract; however, I quickly determined they were incorrect about things they were doing. During the second week of my employment, I was in a meeting with all parties involved. When asked my opinion, I stated what I thought was the truth. I based my findings on data analysis, documentation, and experience. Many of my results did not support the people who hired me, but I felt it was more important for the organization to be told the truth. This didn't sit well with the group who hired me, so they terminated my contract a couple of days later. Even though I was upset, I kept my integrity. However, what upset me the most was that the recruiting company that hired me was trying not to pay me, and I didn't have enough money to check out of the hotel to get home. No way could I leave Houston without getting paid. Fortunately, I received the money to check out of the hotel, but I had to stay with relatives until I received the earnings that were owed to me. Although it took a couple of days, I got paid; thus, God is good. I was able to go back home with money to take care of my family. This was the *sixth* test.

Integrity means a great deal to God. Proverbs 10:9 says, *"People with integrity walk safely, but those who follow crooked paths will be exposed."* Proverbs 28:6 says, *"Better to be poor and honest than to be dishonest and rich."* Finally, Proverbs 11:3 states, *"Honesty guides good people; dishonesty destroys treacherous people."* As hard as it may be as times, integrity is always the best way. God will support it.

Wait on God

When I got back home from Houston, I talked to one of the managers who showed interest in hiring me. I asked him if the opportunity still existed. He said things looked good and told me I should apply. I thought this would be great because it was close to my house, the contract would be directly signed to my company, and it would last for quite a while. Besides, it was paying well. Since this was a government contract at the city level, I had to make sure I took care of any potential organizational issues. When it was time for the city council members to vote on whether to use my services, they didn't approve it. I was agitated because it was suggested this would be only a formality. However, I found out they wanted me to work independently of other companies. I also wanted this, as well. I was promised the vote would come up again next month, so be patient. While it was difficult to wait, I didn't have a choice. During this period, I worked on musical projects, continued lining up other interviews, and stayed in prayer. I had to have faith even when I was feeling the financial pressure. It is essential to wait on God and not move strictly on our own power. Isaiah 40:31 says, *"But those who trust in the Lord will find new strength. They will soar high on wings like eagles. They will run and not grow weary. They will walk and not faint."* Lamentations 3:25 states, *"The Lord is good to those who depend on him, to those who search for him."* Depending and waiting for God takes a level of maturity. When we react to things without His blessing, we miss out on God's best.

Working without the power of God limits our ability to be the best we can be, thus limit our ability to live with maximum opportunity and return on investment.

When the city council voted again, they approved my contract! I was elated, to say the least! The salary was just what I needed, and I couldn't have asked for a better situation. I waited on God, and it worked. I looked at this as an early holiday gift!

Gratitude

After the contract ended in October of 2015, November was an uncertain time. I was trying to take advantage of a business opportunity, where we could make a tremendous profit for the holidays. Unfortunately, I wasn't able to make it happen because of the timing. The company I was partnering with was not ready either, even though they gave me the impression they were. When the deal broke down, I felt the pressure of not having enough cash flow to sustain our lifestyle. Even with cash flow pressures, I still had to continue working on finishing school. The assignments and my dissertation were becoming more difficult and time-consuming as I was getting closer to completion. Completion consisted of finishing all classes and projects in addition to my dissertation.

November 2015 was the last month of classes that weren't associated with my dissertation, and I passed them with flying colors. I could now fully commit to writing my dissertation. I thank God for the support of Lisa through this period in my life because it made me feel everything was going to be alright.

Thanksgiving 2015 turned out to be great. We visited Lisa's, Aunt Ethel, who was in the hospital. There were many family members at the hospital and lots of food. It was great not to think about my situation but to fellowship with others. December 2015 was more of the same. Since the information technology industry was shut down for the year, I spent time planning for the coming new year. I continued working on my dissertation, which was now taking up most of my time. I quickly started to see why most people are not PHDs. I also appreciated the level of time and work that is required to complete a doctorate degree. Even though I was under financial stress, I learned to have complete faith in God and wait on Him to move. It's not that I forgot about faith earlier in life, but I was financially free for many years, and there was a sense of "rest." Now, if I wanted to be successful, I had to rely on *Him*. This creates a different commitment level to God and his word.

Music projects, however, were going well. I was busy producing three albums. Each project was generating income, so I was *grateful* and *blessed* to have the work. Two of the three projects were for artists outside of SoundsOfSunrise. The third artist was part of the SoundsOfSunrise family. Even though I was feeling the stress of working many hours, I was sustaining the family, and Lisa was supportive. The children were aware revenue was not the way it used to be. Two of them were actively looking for jobs. I felt this was healthy because it was time the financial responsibility was distributed. I was getting older and in today's culture of laying off older workers, shifting to a family culture where all people in the family work was necessary.

While Christmas was good because the family was together, January started out with a different feeling. There was plenty of work to do. My dissertation needed to be finished. There were two album productions and a single that was scheduled for release. I was approached to start a new church album. Finally, many promotional projects needed to be started. These projects were generating income, and there was a chance to get more projects in the future. However, I didn't have the bandwidth to do anything else. Also, mentally, I was starting to feel the weight of changes and attitudes with one of our children.

I needed to figure out a different strategy on how to generate enough revenue to make ends meet. God worked it worked, so two of my sons were still working after the holidays.

They were able to keep their jobs, and that was a blessing. Even though one of them didn't particularly care for their current job situation, they hung in there and stayed applying for another position. The other son liked what they were doing, so it was a good situation. My child that wasn't working needed personal money that we still weren't in a position give them as much as they would have liked. However, God always gave us what we needed.

We need to be grateful for how God blesses us. Thessalonians 5:18 states, *"Be thankful in all circumstances, for this is God's will for you who belong to Christ Jesus."* Hebrews 12:28 says, *"Since we are receiving a Kingdom that is unshakable, let us be thankful and please God by worshiping him with holy fear and awe."*

Later in the year, a SoundsOfSunrise project was released in August of 2017 and was very well received. I thought the mixing was a little rushed, but overall, people enjoyed the music quite a bit. We also had a release party. There was standing room only, and it was well-received. It was great to play live the songs we worked on in the studio. The singers and musicians enjoyed the event, and the plan was to do more of them. Lisa was very supportive, and so was the rest of the family. While there were financial issues concerning us, God sustained us, and we were holding on to His grace on our lives. Through all the problems, I was up for the challenge and was grateful for what He had done for us. *Deuteronomy 26:11 says, "Afterward you may go and celebrate because of all the good things the Lord your God has given to you and your household...."* God wants us to be in His perfect will for our lives. For us to be truly blessed, we must want the same.

Gratitude lets God know we adore Him and what He has done in our lives. Think about how it makes you feel when people are grateful for what you've done for them. I know it makes me feel loved and appreciated. I believe God feels the same way when we show Him gratitude. Psalm 118:24 (ESV) tells us, *"This is the day the Lord has made. We will rejoice and be glad in it."* Hebrews 12:28 states, *"Since we are receiving a Kingdom that is unshakable, let us be thankful and please God by worshiping him with holy fear and awe."* Gratitude is manifested when our hearts turn towards emulating God's heart.

It becomes evident to others as a fruit of the spirit. When we empty ourselves of ourselves and become filled with the Holy Spirit, gratitude is witnessed, and strongholds are broken.

Brokenness

Divine sovereignty vs. human responsibility

Again, I didn't see the brokenness, and what I call the "*Job Test*" that was about to happen…. In June 2017, I was finishing the music portion of the label project and began the mixing phase. This was also a good feeling because once this project was complete, I could focus on teaching and getting into the next step of generating more revenue. God was working in our lives and sustaining us despite our lack of money. My real concern was the attitude of one of my children. Due to possible health concerns, we took them to the doctor's office, and medical experts could find nothing wrong. They were looking for potential issues that could affect the lungs, heart, and other parts of the body. They concluded anxiety was the problem partly due to the financial stress. I felt responsible for this, but I had no control over the situation. I knew everything was in God's hands, and the most I could do was to do my part. This leads to the question; *how can we be responsible for things we have no control over?* This becomes an issue of God's divine sovereignty versus personal responsibility. At the end of the day, the Lord will carry out his plan according to his purpose. This can be perplexing because if we are out of alignment with his will, it doesn't matter what we do, even if we are very responsible. Job 42:2 tells us, *"I know that you can do anything, and no one can stop you."* Without understanding God's purpose, this can lead to frustration, depression, and brokenness. Psalm 135:6, *"The Lord does whatever pleases him throughout all heaven and earth, and on the seas and in their depths."* God is indeed sovereign and the ruler over all things. He designs every detailed process and instance of this truth. However, this creates a considerable dilemma. While God is sovereign, man *still* has responsibility and power over decision making. When we come face to face with the coexistence of divine severity versus human responsibility, we lack deeper scriptural understanding, thus creating internal conflicts, which can lead to brokenness. Isaiah 46:9-10 states, *"Remember the things I have done in the past. For I alone am God! I am God, and there is none like me. Only I can tell you the future before it even happens. Everything I plan will come to pass, for I do whatever I wish."* If people are ultimately responsible for their actions to freedom of choice or issues that occur in life and God is sovereign, what is the reconciliation? Why does God lead us to brokenness?

God's Will

God chooses people for His particular purposes in the outworking of His plan. Jeremiah 1:5 says, *"I knew you before I formed you in your mother's womb. Before you were born, I set you apart and appointed you as my prophet to the nations."* This tells us God will set us apart when we are his own, regardless of our thoughts or plans. Finally, God's plan and desires are contrasting facets of His will. He shows His aspiration regarding what men should do, but His specific plan for what men *will* do is concealed. People don't understand how God reconciles these two facets together in His mind. I believe brokenness leads to being molded into the person God wants us to be to carry out the purpose he has for our lives. Brokenness is a complicated process. Galatians 2:20 says, *"My old self has been crucified with Christ. It is no longer I who live, but Christ lives in me. So, I live in this earthly body by trusting in the Son of God, who loved me and gave himself for me."*

By this time, other people in the family were working. This helped a great deal because financial responsibility was being distributed to everyone. While I didn't want the children that were working to be locked into helping financially, it was required to keep the family together. This hurt me significantly, but I knew God was working through all the issues, and his grace was on us. I *had* to hold on to that belief.

Physically the long hours were taking a toll me, so I took a break from projects and unnecessary things. This was tough to do but necessary. I knew I had to make more money, but I also had to put my family and health first. I had to live by the Holy

Spirit and faith, not by fear. I continued teaching and resting. It was a pleasure to plan lectures and teach my students. I continued to grow as a professor and looked forward to teaching additional classes.

October has always been a special month for our family. Both Lisa and I have birthdays in October. Our anniversary is also in October. Finally, one of our sons had a birthday in October as well. He was becoming an accomplished photographer, writer, and film buff. My other son was becoming a musical artist. It was exciting for me to see him learning to play the piano, write, and produce music. My daughter was singing, acting, dancing, and playing basketball. I enjoyed watching them all develop their talent and skills. Again, God's plan will prevail.

The problems didn't go away, however. We still were having financial issues, but I *rested* in knowing God had our backs. I knew if we were aligned with his purpose and put faith in action, we would be alright. I also began to work on the church album project. I thought it would be best to work on a single first and then develop the rest of the album later. This approach also gave me a chance to properly think through the process and really understand what was needed to proceed. In November 2017, I continued to work on the church single. This was an exciting process because of my approach. I was trying to take a song that was familiar to the congregation but with a unique and updated flair. I also started teaching a new class. This class was not special needs, but a senior high school class.

I thought this was interesting because the focus shifted away from college students and shifted towards high school students interested in dual enrollment. The first vocational class I taught focused on providing students with the necessary tools and skills for them to create a "blueprint" for the workplace.

The topics covered include, but were not limited to, self-discovery, time management, job market realities, workplace skills (in-depth), effective communication, contacting employers, preparing for the interview, getting hired, and keeping your job. Each week there were two topics covered. The second vocational class was a blueprint for customer service. This course was designed to provide new and incumbent workers with the customer service skills required to get to know their customers or client and to increase their employability. The topics covered but were not limited to understand what customers want, listening to customers, and telephone customer service. After completing this course, the student had an option to continue their education or become gainfully employed. The third class focused on job search strategies. The course was designed to provide prospective employees with a support system that could assist them in preparation for the workforce. The topics covered but were not limited to: planning their job search, utilizing outside resources, the "hidden" job market, and job market research. The fourth course was designed to provide new and incumbent workers with the knowledge to increase their level of customer service and colleague relations. The topics covered included the new employee, understanding the workplace culture, and dealing with change. I learned a great deal from my students and incorporated what I learned into my syllabi.

  I also completed the church single. I planned to release it in the upcoming new year. I was happy to celebrate my son's birthday and my daughter's birthday. My son was delighted that we invited friends and family to play basketball. My daughter was pleased to have a good time with her friends and family also. She turned 16, and with everything we were going through, I thought it was the right thing to do. The end of the month was focused on family, friends, and the birth of Christ. God is still in control, and he was protecting us though all the circumstances of life.

Rock Bottom

This was the period where my youngest child was continuing to struggle with situations she was going through, regarding our financial struggles. She was having physical problems as well. Many times, we would take her to the doctor's office and hospitals. Anxiety came up multiple times as a factor. At the time, I didn't know what contributed to the tension, but I later found out some of it was because of inconsistent revenue. It was tough to see my child suffering due to something that was not her fault. I felt God can test me, but why were *other* family members being included? It seemed unfair and was very challenging to watch.

I will never waiver from my belief in God. Again, I've experienced too many times how he protected and guided us. Although we were not aware of all the outside influences affecting her during this period, we could see she needed help. This was additionally frustrating because she didn't discuss with me what she was really going through. I went through many emotions regarding this matter and felt helpless. I was praying for clarity, resolution, and healing. Even though the money was still scarce, God took care of us.

By this time, as stated before, I knew He had us on a specific path and direction; therefore, I was past worrying and freaking out about issues that came my way. By this time, there were so many things being done to bridge the money gap, such as selling musical equipment from my studio, eliminating excess bills, simplifying our lifestyle, and working on increasing revenue without creating extra stress. All of this was done with prayer and listening to the Holy Spirit. After many times going to see doctors for various things, they suggested counseling. After much discussion, we decided to take her to see a counselor. We did have some apprehension because it wasn't Christian counseling. We asked the doctor could we use the church counselors, but they felt it was insufficient. I don't know the exact reason for this, but what I was told the level of help required needed to be geared more towards mental and psychological rather than spiritual counseling. Although we felt Christian counseling would work, we had to take the advice of the professionals. I knew we were entering into another phase.

The Problem of Suffering

Counseling for my daughter didn't seem to work, and we were at a loss. Things happening during this period that was out of the norm for us, and we had to resolve the situation. This was beyond the financial problems, and either we were being tested, or the spiritual attacks were getting stronger. I believe it could have been a combination of both. Since it was becoming difficult to talk to people about the ordeal, I also began counseling. I felt if there were something I could do to change myself, I would be able to help others.

I also felt the stress of the financial situation could have caused others to have phycological difficulties, not just my daughter. We were entering a dark period. Even though God was with us, family tenseness continued to increase. While God was providing for our needs, there was a sense of stress in the family. I believe the family wanted a sense of relief. However, God was bringing out things that stayed dormant for many years. Things were tense, and we stayed in constant prayer. This was a period where there were many conversations about things that were on the minds of family members. This was very interesting and painful at the same time. Our children were grown by this time, and some felt more comfortable talking about things that occurred in their lives that were not aware of. I believe this was God's way of allowing family members to enter a cleansing period. It was a form of *"therapy."* Although the conversations were insightful, it was difficult to rein them in from an *"emotional"* point of view. I think this was due to the *"rawness"* and *"honesty."* God still knew how to keep the family cohesive in a very candid and emotional environment.

There were more conversations, and they became more in-depth. I was finding out personality traits I didn't know existed. This was quite surprising because what I thought was the case was far from the truth. Some things were disturbing to see and hear while others were great. Despite this, it was good for us to go through the process because we were not the same people we were years ago. We *all* needed to understand everyone's physiologies to embrace or not embrace them.

In terms of finding work, September 2018 was a month that saw me become even more frustrated. Work insistency was really getting to me, and I felt helpless. It didn't matter how many resumes I would send out or interviews I'd go on. I couldn't find anything. What made things worse is that the last few years were weighing on my mind in a way that prevented me from being productive. During this period in the past, I was always productive even though the difficulty. I was now beginning to feel like a punch-drunk prizefighter. I wasn't working on a musical project, I didn't have a class to teach, couldn't find work and was swimming in the deep water at home. What made things even worse is that I finished counseling, and my counselor determined there were no mental issues. Under any other circumstance, this would be great news, but in my situation, I was desperately trying to find something to *"pin"* this situation on. I had been through so many tests at this point, and to have my family see me in a helpless state was the worst feeling in the world.

I was starting to have a crack in my faith, and I knew I couldn't let that happen. I didn't have time to feel sorry for myself. I had to lead not only my family, but I had to lead the worship arts team, with a smile on my face. I knew this was another "*Job Test*," but the real question was, why?

By October 2018, I began falling into a depression. This was the first time in my life I really thought about dying. I was getting tired of this fight and wondered if the family would be better without me. I didn't talk about it to anyone because I still had to lead, and I couldn't put my burdens on them. Depression is a silent killer, and it's right where Satan wants us to be. Even though I knew better, I couldn't see a way out. Usually, when I'd get to this point, God's grace was enough, or he would provide precisely when it was really required. This time I didn't see the *door*, and I was getting tired. I was hearing about many of my friends in poor health or dying. One thing was for sure, I didn't want that on my legacy.

Even though I couldn't do much for Lisa's or Alex's birthday, I spent time with them. Again, I didn't have a lot of money for our anniversary, but we spent time together. In looking back, I think God was forcing us to deal with each other in a way we never did before. This was not easy, and it certainly was tense with drama. But as my son often said, *"healing can be messy and time-consuming."* I held on to these thoughts while trying to still hold on to faith in God's Word. What I was really concerned about was the family situation. After many discussions, there were still many issues that needed to resolve. Though most of us were committed to making things better, it was still an issue regarding how to make that happen. Besides, everyone was not confined to forgiveness. In the situation, everyone needed to commit to reconciliation. However, we could not force that to happen. It had to be done with *"God softening the hearts of people.*" Many times, when we were close to getting a breakthrough, somebody would speak, or something would happen to cause reconciliation from not happening. God cannot work in this type of environment, and I knew that. All I could do was pray for hearts to change.

We would begin to make progress, but most times, conversations resulted in discord. It was starting to become aware to me that if most of the discontentment centered around my layoff in 2013. Even though God had his plan for us, there seemed to be a considerable cost. I didn't know how much longer this level of discord could continue.

It was becoming apparent to me, we had to do more than just talking about the loss of my job. Things were going on that went back years before my layoff in June 2013. If the family was to move forward together, it was imperative to be open, and honestly discuss all issues, regardless of how painful.

The next month things were still tense, but there was an attempt to reconcile. While the conversations were difficult, we were still talking. I know God was working jobs out, but I wish it were easier. Our family needed some relief in the worst way. The years of financial difficulty had worn the family down. We are a Christian family and needed God's touch.

In May, the family situation came to a breaking point. There were things said or occurred that created a very memorable event. At the time, I thought it was the worst thing that happened to us, but looking back, it was the beginning of getting to the root of problems that existed long before the year 2013. We were now dealing with things we never dealt with before as a family. Everyone was trying to figure out how did we get to this place. Even though a couple of people needed additional space to get a better understanding of where they were personally, the rest of us worked together collectively. This led to many conversations to resolve deep-rooted problems. God has a funny way of allowing things to get worse before they get better. During this time, we were *"in the wild."*

July 2019 was a time of prayer and deep self-reflection. I believe this was the darkest time we've ever had as a family. Most families would have been taken down, but God was protecting us. Lisa and I were on vacation from teaching, so we spent many hours thinking about what each other did wrong and discussed how we can make it right for everyone. This self-reflection was totally needed. With the help of God, the family was spending time talking *"to"* each other, not *"at"* each other. There were many nights we would stay up and talk about what we need to do to move forward.

God breaks us down so He can build us up to promote His purpose. He wants us to entirely rely on Him and no one else. Deuteronomy 8:3 says, *"Yes, he humbled you by letting you go hungry and then feeding you with manna, a food previously unknown to you and your ancestors. He did it to teach you that people do not live by bread alone; rather, we live by every word that comes from the mouth of the Lord."* Although David in the bible was a man after God's own heart. However, it took ten years of being torn down and stripped of just about everything. James 4:7 says, *"So humble yourselves before God. Resist the devil, and he will flee from you."*

God Provides For Our Needs
(Joshua 1:1-7)

Restoration

January 2018 started off with optimism, but real-life issues were real. I finished my fall 2017 class, which I enjoyed very much and was preparing to start teaching my spring 2018 class in February. We released the church single, which generated a great response oversees. I was recuperating from producing projects during the previous year and escaped the ills of burnout. However, because of the lack of enough stable revenue (at the time I didn't know the reason for the changes of emotion and personality), as stated earlier, my youngest child was increasingly showing the signs of being affected by the situation. I knew that God was protecting, guiding, molding, and preparing our family for his purpose, but how do you tell this to a child this who is feeling unloved? What made this increasingly difficult was the communication was breaking down. Finally, the worship arts pastor at church stepped down. These issues would be a driving theme and set the tone for the year.

The new class started Spring Semester 2018 was with students that attended a charter school. Students that attend the school were looking for an alternative way of learning. Some students left the public school system for various reasons. Others felt they could get a more personal education attending a charter school. I was up for the challenge. Many students came from adverse backgrounds. I embraced being part of helping them transfer into the adult working world. I created a specific syllabus designed to give them support and education by providing a creative and interactive learning environment. I enjoyed working with my students. Since many of them had personal issues, it was a challenge to get through to them. To gain their trust, I listened to their stories. I was genuinely moved to talk to them. I was committed to helping in any way I could. Listening to their requests, I decided to create field trips for them so they could see things and meet people that are aligned with their interests.

I received unexpected news at the end of January 2018. The worship arts pastor at whom I worked with for many years at church stepped down. I knew it would be hard to manage his loss. I also knew there would be people trying to fill the void of power. Although I knew this was normal in secular organizations, I wasn't ready to see the level at which this played out in the church. It became increasingly clear to me behind closed doors, there wasn't too much of a difference, and I believed this was unfortunate. With the departure of our worship arts pastor, I felt an additional weight on my shoulders. There were only a couple of people who could help fill the void in leadership and talent. I worked closely with those people the church leadership asked me to work with. Although it was difficult, we filled the void, and the congregation didn't notice a drop in quality. While there were some songs, we didn't have the voices to sing, they were replaced with songs others could do. At the beginning of the departure, the church was concerned there would be a loss of quality and leadership, but I knew that would not be the case. It took a little while for them to see, we could continue without major problems, but eventually, their confidence in us was realized. The church released church single was successful. The song was streaming in over 15 countries. I was surprised Asia was actively listening. I thought it was encouraging to have a diverse listening audience. Driven by the excitement of the early response, I quickly began to plan to work on the rest of the album. I set up meetings and wrote plans. I had about 30 songs in mind. I felt if I recorded the top 20 songs, we'd be ok. I was still trying to rest from getting involved with too many projects. I felt burnout seeping in due to years of working on many musical projects, working on my doctorate, and the stress of inconsistent work. I knew my health was not bad, but If I was to keep strong, I needed somewhat of a break. Many people told me I was somewhat of a workaholic, and I finally began to listen and take heed. Even with what I was doing, my plate was full. I also knew God intended for us to rest.

    I continued working on the church album but had an idea to do a video to help the plight of homelessness. In Southern California, homelessness is a big problem. According to the U.S. Department of Housing and Urban Development (HUD), California had approximately 129,972 experiencing homelessness as of January 2018. The issue of homelessness affects 58 counties in California. The causes of homelessness are due to issues such as job loss, lack of affordable housing, drug and alcohol abuse, and physical and mental illness. The purpose of the video was to shed light on this issue and create an environment to generate revenue to help assist homeless shelters in providing solutions for people in need of housing, medical assistance, mental diagnosis, vocational education, jobs, food, and spiritual guidance.

Trusting in God leads to lives being transformed. Romans 12:2 says, "Do not be conformed to this world, but be transformed by the renewal of your mind, that by testing you may discern what is the will of God, what is good and acceptable and perfect." 2 Corinthians 3:18 says, "And we all, with unveiled face, beholding the glory of the Lord, are being transformed into the same image from one degree of glory to another. For this comes from the Lord, who is the Spirit." Finally, Romans 5:1-6 states, *"Therefore, since we have been made right in God's sight by faith, we have peace with God because of what Jesus Christ our Lord has done for us. Because of our faith, Christ has brought us into this place of undeserved privilege where we now stand, and we confidently and joyfully look forward to sharing God's glory. We can rejoice, too, when we run into problems and trials, for we know that they help us develop endurance. And endurance develops strength of character, and character strengthens our confident hope of salvation. And this hope will not lead to disappointment. For we know how dearly God loves us because he has given us the Holy Spirit to fill our hearts with his love. When we were utterly helpless, Christ came at just the right time and died for us sinners."*

Chapter 4

Standing on Faith

Staying positive

July 2013 was great! Lisa and I continued working on planning our family reunion in Indio, California. It felt great to know people were coming from different parts of the country. I treated them to a weekend at the Terra Lago Resort, which made me feel good. The family loved being together, and I really needed to spend quality time enjoying everyone's company. I was also swamped planning the new SoundsOfSunrise album, titled "I Believe." When the month of August began, I was still in good spirits. Even though it was going into the 2nd month of not being employed, there were enough savings to sustain our family. I received the severance pay from SAP, so money was not an issue. I continued to work on the "I Believe" music project. I was building the business and was even contemplating running my business fulltime. After all, being in business fulltime has so many advantages to it. Having a successful business would allow me to spend more time with the family, not have to be concerned about layoffs, and set my own hours. This was important to me because working on my doctorate was a demanding process. Besides, planning for the family reunion was fun! While thinking through all this, I was still submitting resumes and going on interviews. During this time, I always felt I could be selective because of my qualifications, education, and experience. By the end of the month, I always thought I had time, so I was not concerned, because I was "protected by God." September began where August ended. We had fun during the Labor Day holiday, music projects were going great, still had money, and the family was happy. Even without having a job, the business was expanding. However, I was realistic, so I again went on interviews and submitted resumes. While I didn't feel a real sense of urgency, yet, I began to feel the process was taking a little longer than it needed to. Even with all of this, I knew God was protecting my family, business, our household. I kept reminding myself, *"God protects his own, and I am his favorite."* I thought I was doing the right things, such as giving back to the church with my talent and spending time in the Word. I was a father that was "present" and a faithful husband. I didn't drink, smoke, gamble, do drugs, or abuse my family. I would say to myself, "I'm not inflicting any damage to myself, so God will take care of us. He's done it before, and he will do it again. My faith in God's purpose remained strong. Hebrews 11:1 says the following, *"Now faith is the assurance of things hoped for, the conviction of things not seen."*

Putting on the Armor of God

October was a great month because the family reunion was finally here, and yes, I got a contract through my business! I won a contract working for Chico's retail stores in Fort Myer, Florida. The pay was great, and I said, "Thank you, God!". I felt my prayers were answered, and I was back to work! This made the family reunion even more special.

The family had so much fun and enjoyed each other's company. Although the weather was hot, it really wasn't too bad. Lisa gave Terrance (her nephew) a tribute. He really appreciated it. This was extra special to me because I didn't know he was fighting cancer. I enjoyed my conversations with Terrence, and we had a lot in common. Once the family reunion was over, I shifted my efforts to start work in Fort Myers, FL. I stood on God's Word and remained faithful. Although the contract ended prematurely, I came to the realization it was best to continue working on my doctorate and musical projects.

After the holidays, while I was healing from the death of my mother, I was still looking for work. It was tough when thoughts of her passing would enter my psyche, but I relied on my faith in God's word to keep me in good spirits. It was then when God's Spirit led me to investigate investments I had forgotten about to keep revenue coming in. I discovered I had money saved in a bank account I was unaware of. I also had stocks I forgot about. This helped us get through this period and gave me peace of mind. Even though I knew I had to keep looking, God sustained us again. God let us know he was in control.

I attended my residency in February for the third and final time. I drove to Phoenix, AZ. Even though I had to make sure my dissertation was ready to submit for committee approvals, I took the time to enjoy myself. Working on a Doctorate degree is very intense and time-consuming. However, studying and doing research on a topic that you are passionate about is very rewarding. Most people in the residency were in their third year. I made many friends and connections.

I also finished the mastering of the "I Believe" project. The album came out great. The project took over two years to complete. Although industry people were telling me to break the project up into two separate albums, I listened to the Holy Spirit. When I tried to divide it, there was no *"anointing,"* so I decided to keep it together. It is critical to listen to the Holy Spirit. I wisely made the decision not to go against what the Holy Spirit tells you to do. Once the master was complete, I began to prepare for SoundsOfSunrise to perform live at the Mayor's concert.

God was blessing our family, and things were going well at home. We were catching up on bills and feeling some breathing room. Lisa enjoyed me being able to come home for lunch, and I liked it also. I continued to successfully work on my dissertation. My GPA was excellent, and my committee was pleased. With things going so well, I was praying for the political issues to get better. While God was a blessing to our family, I believe He was also getting us ready for the next *"Job Test."* It was critical to keep on the Armor of God. Ephesians 6:14 says, *"Stand your ground, putting on the belt of truth and the body armor of God's righteousness."*

It is imperative to understand we are in a battle with Satan for our souls. Without full protection against that level of power and attack, we are helpless. Paul tells us how to protect ourselves in Ephesians 6:10-20, which says, *"A final word: Be strong in the Lord and in his mighty power. Put on all of God's armor so that you will be able to stand firm against all strategies of the devil. For we are not fighting against flesh-and-blood enemies, but against evil rulers and authorities of the unseen world, against mighty powers in this dark world, and against evil spirits in the heavenly places. Therefore, put on every piece of God's armor so you will be able to resist the enemy in the time of evil. Then after the battle, you will still be standing*

firm. Stand your ground, putting on the belt of truth and the body armor of God's righteousness. For shoes, put on the peace that comes from the Good News so that you will be fully prepared. In addition to all of these, hold up the shield of faith to stop the fiery arrows of the devil. Put on salvation as your helmet, and take the sword of the Spirit, which is the word of God. Pray in the Spirit at all times and on every occasion. Stay alert and be persistent in your prayers for all believers everywhere. And pray for me, too. Ask God to give me the right words so I can boldly explain God's mysterious plan that the Good News is for Jews and Gentiles alike. I am in chains now, still preaching this message as God's ambassador. So pray that I will keep on speaking boldly for him, as I should."

Determination and staying the course

I started out the year 2016 with high confidence. I had to find work, and things were getting tough financially. We were in a situation now where there wasn't any income, and we were concerned. This was the time when food was becoming scarce, and we started relying on credit cards to eat. There were days where we didn't know how we were going to eat or pay bills. Some days we would count pennies. I could tell I lost weight. I decided to stop depending, looking for work from employers, and began to look for music production projects. It is essential to understand something: even with the lack of food and money, God took care of us. Our water, gas, cordless phone, and utility bills were still getting paid. Every time (even up to the hour), when something was scheduled to be shut off, God came through in many ways. It really taught me not to worry and *just have faith*.

In February 2016, I continued working on my dissertation. I found the literature review section to be exhausting. The research required to produce a quality paper is immense. Once the reading and digesting of the study are at a certain point, writing the essay must be totally original and make sense. In a doctoral dissertation, the first three chapters must be completed before the committee gives the student QRM (Quality Review Methods) approval, and I was now ready to submit my dissertation for approval. When the submission response came back, I was told my paper needed revisions, and this frustrated me. Keep in mind, each correction required me to go back and rewrite 20-30 pages of the document. However, when I began to talk to other doctoral candidates, they told me this was normal. I soon understood that being part of the doctoral community was extraordinary, and other doctorates wanted to make sure candidates were mentally ready and worthy of being part of it. This made me more determined than ever. Nehemiah 6:9 says, *"They were just trying to intimidate us, imagining that they could discourage us and stop the work. So I continued the work with even greater determination."* 1

Corinthians 9:26-27 states, *"So I run with purpose in every step. I am not just shadowboxing. I discipline my body like an athlete, training it to do what it should. Otherwise, I fear that after preaching to others, I myself might be disqualified."*

By April 2016, I was working on making the requested modifications to my dissertation. By now I knew better not to complain about anything, I just got it done. Even though the adjustments were turning into a rewrite, I diligently stayed with it knowing I didn't have an option if I planned on finishing. Again, God was testing, blessing, and providing His grace. In May, my dissertation was coming along well. There were still many revisions to be made and not enough time in the day to get them done. I had to discipline myself regarding time. For example, I would work from nine AM to three PM on my music projects, take an hour break, and put another three hours in. I would then spend six to seven hours working on my dissertation. Travel wasn't a problem because all the work was being done in my studio/office at home. Every now and then I would go outside to get fresh air or go to the store to get away for a while. The thing about working from home is that you are home all the time. Sometimes it is healthy to get out of the house. When I was traveling every week, I didn't want to leave the house when I got home. Again, this is where the discipline comes into play.

As I said earlier, I also worked on multiple music projects to provide income. While it was difficult staying up at night, I was still having fun. It is rewarding to know you are totally working for yourself. It was also good to know Lisa was supporting and encouraging the decision. That removed a lot of pressure from me. It also helped me to continue. There were some internal struggles with individual projects. It was somewhat hard for me to stand behind some of the artists I was producing. Most had specific directions, and that was a good thing. However, I felt I wasn't aligned with some of them. Because of this misalignment, I knew I was producing artists for the wrong reasons. I'm not saying I did it for the money only, but If I weren't getting paid, I wouldn't have produced those projects. I was also completing vocals and working on finalizing the musical tracks on the label project. I had a feeling good about the state of the album and was ready to get to the final stages. Even though I knew things were stressful, God was blessing us and kept us safe.

After three revisions to my dissertation, I finally received QRM approval. This was the big push so can graduate in 2017. If they pass me through, the next step would be to submit to the Institutional Review Board. The Institutional Review Board or IRB for short maintains a Human Research Protection Program to protect the rights and welfare of those persons who volunteer to participate in the research activities of our faculty, students, and staff.

The IRB acts as a regulatory oversight group committed to promoting the ethical and responsible treatment of volunteer human participants in a research study. The IRB performs ethical reviews of research studies to ensure research compliance with all federal, state, and local regulations as well as all institutional policies and procedures in addition to offering education and guidance related to human subject research for the University community. Once I earned IRB acceptance, I could collect data. I was excited about being able to advance in my goal of achieving a doctorate. Despite the trials and tribulations, God was protecting and blessing us the entire time.

Many people don't make it this far, and to get to the IRB phase, let me know this was very close to happening. This would have made my parents proud. I was hoping and praying my children would be proud also. It was important for me to show them they could achieve anything they put their mind to doing.

In December 2016, I was ready for IRB submission. Forms were filled out and submitted. It was critical for this to get done as quickly as possible. I knew I could not move on to collect data until I received IRB approval. In January 2017, I received IRB approval and was now able to start the data gathering process. Getting information together for my dissertation to get IRB approval was very time-consuming. This was the big push, and I needed to work around the clock. Usually, I would get up early to take family members to work or school. I would then work on musical projects throughout the day. My time frame would usually be from nine AM to seven PM. By this time, I need to take a break. I would take a couple of hours to rest and eat. Once everyone was asleep, I would work through the night on my dissertation. As stated earlier, when I was younger, the schedule wouldn't have bothered me. But that was then, and this was now. I found it tough to keep up with daily. However, if we were to succeed, I didn't have any choice.

In February 2017, I received IRB approval, I was now working on collecting data to perform qualitative analysis. This entailed setting up interviews with people, documenting, cleaning, and organizing each interview. Face-to-face interviews and focus groups were the methods of data collection. Interviews were appropriate because participants could reveal critical viewpoints. Interview questions were semi-structured. Demographics included different ethnicities that exist within each church and a relatively equal number of males and females. An audio device and observation notes captured data from each interview. The objective of the interview questions was to provoke in-depth thought by each participant. Interview questions were consistent for all participants. The data collection process captured deep-rooted perceptions, thoughts, and ideas from each participant, so answers from interview questions were open and honest, without limitations. Results from interviews confirmed what participants thought about topics such as weekly rehearsals, sound quality, the skill of musicians and singers, and the experience of the worship team, song selection, and support of the church leadership about having a quality music program in churches. I was busy interviewing people for the data collection portion of the dissertation. Interviews consisted of 31 participants ranging from 18 to 95 years old, with different ethnicities that existed within each church and an equal number of males and females. Interview questions were consistent for all participants. Interviews occurred over three weeks. All selected participants were contacted via a phone call, text, or email before each interview took place. Each participant was interviewed privately at the church of the participant. There was one phone interview due to the participant being sick. Study participation consisted of orally answering the interview questions openly and honestly. The maximum interview time was 40 minutes. Each participant prepared for a two-hour commitment. An audio device and observation notes collected data from each participant interviewed. Interviews were semi-structured to provoke in-depth thought by each participant. There were 15 interview questions. There was one closing question. Interview questions were consistent for all participants. The wording of each interview question helps the person interviewed to reveal honest thoughts and feelings about the mental framework of the participant.

During June 2017, I received QRF (Quality Review Final) approval. This approval process is similar to QRM but not as stringent. QRF contains chapters one through five, and the abstract. I was now ready for the final step, which was my oral defense.

The oral-defense entailed defending the dissertation in front of the committee members and selected colleagues. My presentation was on July 13th, 2017, and it lasted approximately 25-30 minutes. After my oral defense presentation, I was asked questions regarding the thought process, content, conclusion, and literature review. After a few minutes went past, I was told I passed! This was a relief because six years' worth of work was now coming to an end. My program completion date was July 17, 2017, and the diploma date was July 31, 2017. I was now officially a doctorate!

One of the main reasons I wanted to complete this journey was to show my children that despite obstacles, difficulty, and setbacks If you work hard, stay committed, and focused, you can achieve your goals in life. I thanked God that he allowed me to complete this accomplishment. I felt now I could focus on generating more money and finish the label project.

Through all the trials and issues we were going through, I eventually saw how God was transitioning my mindset by staying the course. Rather than complaining about not having a lot of money, I now know I had everything I needed. He was training me for a bigger purpose; *His purpose*. I now also know I couldn't see what he was doing at the time, but his *grace* protected the family and myself. When God prepares us for more significant purposes, it is hard to deal with the circumstances; however, it is critical to know God blesses His own. We must stay under God's plan and use, *regardless* of the events. We must go forward with God. The scriptures discuss staying the course in Hebrews 12:1-2: *"Therefore, since we are surrounded by such a huge crowd of witnesses to the life of faith, let us strip off every weight that slows us down, especially the sin that so easily trips us up. And let us run with endurance the race God has set before us. We do this by keeping our eyes on Jesus, the champion who initiates and perfects our faith. Because of the joy awaiting him, he endured the cross, disregarding its shame. Now he is seated in the place of honor beside God's throne."* Philippians 1:6 says, *"And I am certain that God, who began the good work within you, will continue his work until it is finally finished on the day when Christ Jesus returns."* 2 Timothy 4:7 says, *"I have fought the good fight, I have finished the race, and I have remained faithful."* Finally, Hebrews 11:6 says, *"....it is impossible to please God without faith. Anyone who wants to come to him must believe that God exists and that he rewards those who sincerely seek him."*

Grace

He is enough

There was plenty of job activity in April 2014. I was going on several interviews with different companies, and things looked like they would turn around. I really felt good about one company. They were actively recruiting me, and this gave me hope. They interviewed me more than five times and assured me of a job. However, each time, in the end, the offer never came, and again nobody seemed to understand why. This left me wondering, was there something I was doing wrong? I was beginning to believe I was the only person unemployed. This was starting to concern me in a way that was not healthy. I felt everyone else was getting work even though they weren't nearly as qualified as myself. This test was beginning to weigh heavy on me. However, I knew God's grace was *'enough.'* 2 Corinthians 12:9 tells us, *"..... "My grace is sufficient for you, for my power is made perfect in weakness."......"* Philippians 4:19 states, *"And this same God who takes care of me will supply all your needs from his glorious riches, which have been given to us in Christ Jesus."* In May, I continued going on interviews. While companies said I would get the job, I received no offers. It became apparent to me that I was supposed to keep moving forward with my business. While jobs were not materializing, the company was moving forward. The "I Believe" project was emerging, and everyone was on board.

I was working feverishly to get my doctorate degree. I was growing by leaps and bounds in my faith. God had another plan, I just didn't know what it was. Despite the uncertainty, Lisa and the kids were very supportive. Jason was about to attend CBU, and CJ was working a great job in Dallas. I felt blessed and happy, knowing God had our backs and was taking care of us. Many times we don't know or understand what God's will is for our lives; however, we must continue to believe that His will is best for us. To achieve our purpose in life, we must trust God has our best interest at heart *even* when we are in the darkest of times. The enemy loves it when he feels we are most vulnerable. The bible says, *"Work hard so you can present yourself to God and receive his approval. Be a good worker, one who does not need to be ashamed and who correctly explains the word of truth."* - 2 Timothy 2:15.

Projects

There was a lot of excitement going into the year of 2015. Working for the city was great. I was developing processes and working with staff members to achieve the results of the city officials. It was great to come back after the holidays energized and ready to impact the lives of the people in our city. I was also planning to attend my doctoral residency and had to get committee approval to move forward. By this time, I knew what I wanted to write about. The name of my dissertation was *"Successful Business Models That Promote the Growth of Churches Through Music."* The focus of my study provided insight into what successful music ministries are doing to help increase congregational membership size. The study included current music ministry business models and cultures. The population focused on pastors, church board members, worship leaders, key congregation members, and essential volunteers from churches with significant growth. The objective of the research was to get an understanding of what successful churches are doing to increase congregational membership size through music, specifically in the Southern California area. The method of choice was qualitative, and the design was an exploratory case study. The literature review section contained references used in the research, and the research question helped the study to explore the characteristics of successful church music programs. I enjoyed doing the research because I was learning so much and could apply this information to my ministry as a music director of a megachurch.

I was also working on the final stages of the "I Believe" project. This was an epic 21 song double album. The "I Believe" project has a target audience of young people from ages 12 through 18. The goal of the project was to bring into light everyday struggles with drug/alcohol abuse, rebellion, peer pressure, cutting, loneliness, sex abuse, and human trafficking. In addition to putting some of the demands of everyday living on the table, the project is written in hopes of providing healing, understanding, and answers through a relationship with Jesus Christ. In terms of other musical projects, I started out working on the project I really wanted to do. This worship leader and recording artist was someone I wanted to work with for quite a while. We worked on putting together 15-20 songs with the notion of selecting the best and most appropriate songs. I wanted to produce music I could feel good about. With the number of projects I was working on, I was too committed to even look for a regular job at this point. Both Lisa and I were working together very well. I did the creative work, and Lisa took care of the business side. In many ways, this brought us together and made us closer. Although Lisa and I were ok with the inability to purchase things like we used to, I wasn't aware one of our children didn't like this. I believe outside influences contributed to this frame of mind. Regardless, we kept doing what God instructed us to do.

I also began working on the new church project. I started gathering information about what type of songs were needed. It was great working with congregation members creating lyrics, listening to their stories, and creating music. I also continued working on the SoundsOfSunrise project. We successfully released one of the outside musical projects. While I was glad it was released, there were some reservations. I wanted to take the project in a different direction, but the artist was insistent on doing it his way. I resisted, but I submitted to the old saying, *"the customer's always right."* This was verification to me that in the future, I should not produce projects that were not aligned with my values, brand, or personal beliefs.

During this time, I worked on my album titled "Scores." The "Scores" album included film tracks from various films. The album was a different direction from previously released SoundsOfSunrise projects. The collection consists of inspirational arrangements such as "Oh Lord You're Beautiful" and darker works like "Into the Prism," which show a broad spectrum of musical styles. There were 19 tracks on the album. The genre was considered classical. Even though these tracks were from previously released movies, I felt it was great to finally release them. I knew I was building the label, and I needed to keep releasing products. It was also important to publish material of my own rather than just releasing projects of others. As I was working on these groups of songs, I said to myself I needed to work on a personal, commercial album. At the time, I didn't have a concept of a purpose, but I wanted to help others in the way. While I was going through the journey, God protected me, and I knew if I waited on him to lead me, the outcome would be good.

Breakthrough

God's hand was guiding and protecting us with His grace. Grace is not earned. Grace is a gift from God. We were doing projects to promote the kingdom. Romans 3:24 says, *"Yet God, in his grace, freely makes us right in his sight. He did this through Christ Jesus when he freed us from the penalty for our sins."* Psalm 84:11 states, *"For the Lord God is our sun and our shield. He gives us grace and glory. The Lord will withhold no good thing from those who do what is right."* According to Jennifer Heeren (2019), the different types of grace are salvation, numerous, forgiveness, new, freedom, and future. The scope of this book is focused on future grace. Future grace says God promised to be with us at all times (Heeren, 2019). The Holy Spirit will guide and prompt us as we go through life. God is inside of us in each moment, and those moments lead to a great future (Heeren, 2019). Although we all go through trials, God is there to help us get through them and make our burdens lighter (Heeren, 2019). Jesus himself spoke of the trials here on earth, but John 16:33 says, *"I have told you all this so that you may have peace in me. Here on earth, you will have many trials and sorrows. But take heart, because I have overcome the world."* Going through hard situations where the future is unknown, it is easier to handle it when we are not alone.

Although God was providing and pushing me into a specific direction, there were issues. Juggling many music projects left me drained. I felt I could not hire people to help because of the lack of equipment. Besides, the money being generated was not enough to pay other people. There were also increasingly disturbing signs. One of our children was suffering. As time went on, this became increasingly worse. April 2017 saw the family working hard to make ends meets. It was becoming difficult to pay bills and make ends meet. Since I was working very hard to complete my doctorate, I didn't have much time to look for work. However, God blessed me with an opportunity to get a breakthrough. A friend from church helped me to get a job as a community college professor. This was precisely what I wanted and needed. Remember, grace is a gift. Grace cannot be earned.

Chapter 5

Hope

There are a few definitions of hope; however, I like to use this one, *"hope is the desire for good things to happen in the future."* When people have a belief in positive things, it keeps them mentally healthy, physically engaged in activities, and spiritually strong. Without hope, people can slip into depression. When we have our faith in God, we have *confidence*, *expectation,* and *desire* for good things to happen in the future.

City contract

As mentioned earlier, in October 2014, during the night of the city council vote, I was very nervous. When the deal came to the floor, there was a lot of debate regarding what was the best direction for the city. When it was my time to talk, I did well. Even though I was nervous,

I told them I had the experience, integrity, and leadership skills to do the job. Finally, when they voted, my contract was approved. I was on an emotional high. I can't describe how important this contract was for our family and business. When we got home, we celebrated! I could have easily panicked and proceeded outside of God's will, but I was determined to walk by faith and not by sight. This meant I would not make sporadic choices and decisions. I made sure I didn't make a move until the Spirit told me to. I learned to be led by the Holy Spirit. I felt relieved to know the search for work was over, at least for now. Again, God showed up! This was the *seventh* test.

November 2014 was filled with excitement, optimism, and high expectations. It was a great feeling and an honor to have the opportunity to help the city achieve its objectives. This also allowed me to catch up on bills, finance the "I Believe" project, and save money. Those first weeks were great. I worked independently gathering requirements and met with people to understand their problems, needs, and desires. The workflow wasn't tricky, and most people were supportive and willing to talk to me. I was also trying the learn the business culture. Homelife was stable, and it felt great to be working again.

There was a new energy in everything I was doing, and I knew God was blessing us. After work, I was talking to a senior official and a senior staff person. The senior official was hosting a musical event. As plans were being discussed, I mentioned to them how I could help to make it better. They were very interested, and I felt anything I could do would help the city. I didn't know the complications that would come with it, but God brought me out of a tough situation and gave me just enough grace to get ready for the next test. I enjoyed a wonderful Thanksgiving and Christmas with my family while learning the job and its' organizational culture. Other parts of my life were also great.

Our family needed this break from all the pressure from the obstacles and "tests" we were dealing with. God gave us space to "breath." In the last two weeks of the month, the city shut down for Christmas, and I was ok with that.

I believe God knows our limits and capabilities better than we do. Going into another holiday like the previous year would have been a bit much for us. We thanked God for bringing us this far, and it was time to rest for a couple of weeks. I thanked God for allowing the year to end how it did. In addition to the city contract, the church eventually decided to start paying me. Although it wasn't much, I was very thankful because I really needed it. Having multiple sources of income helped bridge the financial gap.

Encouragement

I also felt appreciated and encouraged to know the church acknowledged my contribution. People were discussing the newly hired Senior Pastor. I knew this would bring a significant shift in direction. I even knew I needed to be aware of others jockeying for position and power. This indeed was happening. However, I stayed in prayer regarding how to handle it. Since I was a leader in the church, much of the politics was geared towards me, and it made me very uncomfortable. I continued to pray and battle through it. What really surprised me was the extent to which some people would go to try and gain political leverage. In my opinion, that mindset was an abuse of power. After all, this was the church; things like this should not happen. It was quite eye-opening for me. In spite of everything, I was encouraged and hopeful about what God was doing.

For example, the video we shot that was geared to help the homeless was coming along very well. Some scenes were shot at the church. I thought it was great to see so many people come out and participate. Since Easter was coming up, I decided to wait and shoot the other parts of the video after Easter.

I was also encouraged the vocational education college class I taught was going well. My students were learning a lot, and I was happy for them. There was a moment where I wish other students who dropped the class would have stayed. For example, I had a student that was exceptional and very talented in nursing. She had excellent grades. However, she was influenced by outside forces that kept her from realizing her true potential. I talked to her and pleaded with her to stay in the class. She said she would. However, when it was time for her to do the work, she didn't do it and stopped attending classes. I eventually heard she wasn't coming back. The disappointing part is that she earned an A on her test. I could not pass her because she chose not to do the work. I believe this was a loss of opportunity for her. It was a reminder to me we are partially a summation of our choices in life. Matthew 7:13-14 states, *"You can enter God's Kingdom only through the narrow gate. The highway to hell is broad, and its gate is wide for the many who choose that way. But the gateway to life is very narrow, and the road is difficult, and only a few ever find it."*

This was also the first Easter service where the worship pastor of more than fifteen years was not there.

Although the church worship team was doing ok, the exceptional singers with the most talent and expertise were missing. I knew a lot was on my shoulders. This was because not only did I have to make sure the music was excellent, but I also had to make sure the overall service went well. The worship team worked hard to assure the senior-level church management things would be fine.

I continued to work with my students. As mentioned earlier, many of my students in this class had hardships, and they needed extra help and encouragement. Some students also needed assurance and confidence. I decided to set up field trips explicitly designed for their interests and field of study.

you got this

I also worked diligently on the "It's My Time" video. The video team was making plans to shoot the outside scenes in downtown Los Angeles. These shots were going to capture people who were homeless, living on the street in tents. I was very encouraged that our video was helping to put a spotlight on people who do not have a place to live. It is encouraging to know we must help people any way we can, and by helping people, we are showing them, love. By showing people love, we are expressing our love for God. Matthew 25:40-45 says the following, *"And the King will say, 'I tell you the truth when you did it to one of the least of these, my brothers and sisters, you were doing it to me!' "Then the King will turn to those on the left and say, 'Away with you, you cursed ones, into the eternal fire prepared for the devil and his demons. For I was hungry, and you didn't feed me. I was thirsty, and you didn't give me a drink. I was a stranger, and you didn't invite me to your home. I was naked, and you didn't give me clothing. I was sick and in prison, and you didn't visit me.' "Then they will reply, 'Lord, when did we ever see you hungry or thirsty or a stranger or naked or sick or in prison, and not help you?' "And he will answer,*

'I tell you the truth when you refused to help the least of these my brothers and sisters, you were refusing to help me.'"

Being in Christ gives us hope in knowing that our needs will be met. This hope in very encouraging in so many ways. Joshua 1:9 says, *"This is my command—be strong and courageous! Do not be afraid or discouraged. For the Lord, your God is with you wherever you go."* Psalm 121:1-8 states, *"I look up to the mountains—does my help come from there? My help comes from the Lord, who made heaven and earth! He will not let you stumble; the one who watches over you will not slumber. Indeed, he who watches over Israel never slumbers or sleeps. The Lord himself watches over you! The Lord stands beside you as your protective shade. The sun will not harm you by day, nor the moon at night. The Lord keeps you from all harm and watches over your life. The Lord keeps watching over you as you come and go, both now and forever."*

Healing and Transformation

Helping others

As I mentioned previously, I had a great time shooting the "It's My Time" video. It was both educational and fun. I also felt it was an honor meeting people who were homeless and hearing their stories. There were people I met who were brilliant and talented. This experience let me know homelessness could happen to anybody. This brought tremendous healing to me, knowing in spite of my situation, I could help someone else who was in a worse situation. By focusing on the needs of others, I was being healed myself.

There were a couple of exciting occurrences that stuck with me. This first was a homeless person we talked to be a former singer and know our artist. He could also sing very well. It let me know most people are a paycheck or one misfortune away from being homeless themselves. The second occurrence was when we were giving out snack bags to those who were participating in the video. We had approximately 50 bags. When we were passing out bags, more than 200 people lined up to receive them, and we, unfortunately, had to turn them away. Its realty let me know the severity of the problem. My students also came and participated in the video. I used the video shooting as a field trip for them. I thought this was an excellent opportunity for them to see how videos are shot. I was told they enjoyed themselves.

We serve God by helping others. When others help, we allow the Holy Spirit to heal us as well. This spiritual healing helps us to overcome the world we currently live in, and we enter into a mindset of *unselfishness*. God blesses this because when we help others, we are in *oneness* with Him. This oneness with God brings forth healing and transformation. 1 John 4:19-20 says, *"We love each other because he loved us first. If someone says, "I love God," but hates a fellow believer, that person is a liar; for if we don't love people we can see, how can we love God, whom we cannot see?"* Luke 3:10 states, *"... "If you have two shirts, give one to the poor. If you have food, share it with those who are hungry."* Helping others brings purpose to our lives. Through finding real meaning, we are *healed.*

Musical Fulfillment

Although the money was tight during this initial period of producing other artists, Lisa was very supportive. I thanked God every day for her involvement and interest. Lisa and I were beginning to discuss the possibility of going into full-time production. We needed the money, and I had the studio and connections. I felt we could do it if the hourly rate were thought out well. With that being the case, it really made sense to pursue the possibility of doing fulltime production. Confirmation of this came when an artist asked us to produce them. They heard about us in one of the internet advertisements. It was a blessing to get the work. This was the first in a few productions that year. It showed me that producing outside artists had a monetary value. The downside to it was working at night. I quickly realized it was difficult for me to stay up after 1 or 2 AM. When I was younger, this was never an issue, but now, I had to be disciplined. Lisa was instrumental in helping me to organize the operational side of things. This was a big help. It also kept us united as a family in the face of a tight financial situation. While the family was united around the idea of full-time production, I was deep into my dissertation, so I held off sending out resumes unless there was a real opportunity to get an interview. The money coming in from projects was getting a little better, and I cut back on many expenses.

Through this time, we stayed close to God because we knew despite everything that was going on, *He* was providing for us. I can't emphasis this enough. God always came through when we needed him to. We were used to this now, so we stopped worrying about things we had no control over and relied on faith. I could remember not just the month of March, but throughout this period, it would come down to the day or hour when something was about to get cut off, and the provisions arrived. I believe God was testing and providing for us while giving us the grace to continue. At the time, I didn't realize it, but *through His grace, we were all being healed.*

The artists that I was producing during this time were happy, and that made me feel we were on the right path. We still had financial concerns, and there were many bills, but we were united and working together. We knew God was healing us, and that is what kept us going. We released a project from an artist that had different political views from my own. However, we were both Christians and men of God. We were tied together by our spiritual values, so I enjoyed working with him. I also thought he was a good writer. However, I quickly came to the realization these types of projects can be challenging to do because It becomes hard to endorse a plan or an artist that doesn't align with company brands or personal beliefs. I started to rethink what type of projects I would support in the future. Even though revenue is a driving force for being in business, it is more important to do projects consistent with core values. With that being said, the project came out great.

May 2015 started out with the release of the "I Believe" Album. It was well-received by listeners. It was a long project but well worth it. If we could help just one person, it would have been well worth it. I wasn't really concerned about the monetary gain, I was more concerned about who the album would bless. Through the process of writing songs, conducting interviews, producing videos, and talking to people, I learned not only was there a need for this type of project, but it was I knew we would make an impact. One of our crucial SoundsOfSunrise personnel suggested we submit one of our videos titled "Runaway" to KSGN's Spirit West Coast Contest. We thought it was an idea, so I did.

Needless to say, we won, but I'll discuss details later. The church also got behind the album, which helped as well. June 2015 was another good one. Turns out, we won KSGN's Spirit West Coast Opening Act Contest. We got the opportunity to play at Citizen's Bank Arena with TobyMac, Newsboys, Matt Redman, Hillsong Young & Free, Rend Collective, and Mandisa. It was an honor to play with these great artists, and a blessing to know the city and community was behind us. The concert was sold out with over 11,000 people. We knew this was special and could have catapulted us to the next level. Unfortunately, I depleted so much energy to get there I didn't have enough to push any further. I was still dealing with the issues with the city regarding participating in the jazz festival, and I was being drained. With the album successfully released and both concerts over July 2015 was a time for the healing to start. Finally, the Scores album was released the following year in July 2016. I didn't want to put a lot of promotion around it, so it was a quiet release. I made a point to have the album release be calm. I did, however, work on projects that were released in July. I felt good that the project I was working on was successful.

Because I was becoming healed from previous situations I talked about earlier in the book such as death, job loss, etc.. These album releases were very fulfilling. There is great joy in knowing that God brings fulfillment to our lives. When we are fulfilled in God's purpose, not only are we healed, but we start to see God for who He is, which is love. 1 John 3:1-2 says, *"See how very much our Father loves us, for he calls us his children, and that is what we are! But the people who belong to this world don't recognize that we are God's children because they don't know him. Dear friends, we are already God's children, but he has not yet shown us what we will be like when Christ appears. But we do know that we will be like him, for we will see him as he really is."*

December 2016 was an exciting month. The month was partly busy, loving, worshipful, and family-oriented. The song produced for the SoundsOfSunrise Artist was released. It was very well received. During January of 2017, we were planning to put together a promotion strategy to push the soon to be released album. I was also busy working on the other projects where one album was scheduled for release in February 2017. Although I had to work through some of the holidays, I still managed to spend quality time with the family. My family worked many hours each week. It was great to see them doing what was required to help the family financially. They were working many hours and doing a great job contributing. We were able to give each other gifts this year, and I thought this was great.

Every year we make sure we pray and read scripture together each Christmas morning. Despite the issues, we had a lot to be thankful for. God was giving us plenty of grace, and to know He had our backs through this period was worth its' weight in gold. When we are going through difficulties, it is imperative to stay focused on God's word and be in alignment with His purpose for our lives.

Educational Fulfillment

I enjoyed working on my doctorate more than my masters because of the creativity of writing a dissertation. I preferred qualitative research rather than quantitative research. Having a software analysis and design background, it was different for me to perform qualitative research. Besides, writing an exploratory multiple case study was perfect for me. The immediate objective was to flush out the errors, get the literature review, and analysis sections as clean as possible. I quickly found out that the literature review section can make or break a research document.

By using a qualitative methodology to discover the phenomena of successful worship teams, churches that are in decline could expand their congregational membership. The purpose of the exploratory study was to explore best practice approaches of successful church music programs and try to understand what is done to increase congregational membership size through music. Best practices of three megachurches located in the Southern California area were studied. The focus of the research was to explore successful church music programs and business models. The study also attempted to help church leaders understand what can be done to increase congregational membership through music.

The literature review helped the researcher to analyze approaches to church leadership, components of the contemporary worship team, connection between business and the church, educational level of the church staff, volunteers of growing churches, and the importance of music to church members. The literature review revealed how church leaders struggled to implement non-traditional church-based solutions but eventually integrated diverse musical styles. The integration of musical styles made it difficult for churches to integrate their business model strategy concerning music programs. This difficulty was mainly due to a lack of understanding, training, expertise, vision, and resources. Going through this process was also a way of experiencing God's healing power and being fulfilled knowing the dissertation help churches to bring others to Christ through music. 2 Peter 1:2-4 says, *"May God give you more and more grace and peace as you grow in your knowledge of God and Jesus our Lord. By his divine power, God has given us everything we need for living a godly life. We have received all of this by coming to know him, the one who called us to himself by means of his marvelous glory and excellence. And because of his glory and excellence, he has given us great and precious promises. These are the promises that enable you to share his divine nature and escape the world's corruption caused by human desires."*

Employment Transition

August 2017, I started my first class as an adjunct college professor! This was quite exciting because it marked the beginning of my transition from being a traveling consultant to becoming a college professor. My students made the class special. There were nine special needs students in my class. Two students were deaf, one student was blind, and another had learning disabilities. I believe this was a test for me, in that if I could teach students with special needs, it would give me the confidence I needed as a new instructor. I enjoyed working with the students and hearing their stories. As I got to know them, it helped me to build my teaching plan and curriculum for other classes. I also learned about the challenges of people with learning disabilities and special needs. I concluded there needs to be more done to understand the requirements of students who have special needs. They are bright, optimistic, and wonderful students. For example, my students wanted to have careers in law, medicine, paleontology, aeronautics, security, and engineering. It was important for me to give them the inspiration and support they need to pursue their dreams. This was the perfect first class to have. I

In September 2017, I continued working as a college professor, working with my students with special needs. I learned a great deal from my students, and I was instructing them regarding vocational education. Later in the fall, I started teaching my new class. This was a totally different group of students. These students came from public schools. There were a couple of them who felt entitled, but I handled that well. I could academically challenge this class a little more, and I felt empowered and excited about that. It was an accelerated class, so things moved quickly. The students were up for the challenge and embraced the work. I knew this group of students was special, and it felt great working with smart and gifted people.

Lisa also applied to teach again. I was delighted to see her do this. It made me happy that after raising the kids, she was now moving into the next phase of her life. It was also great to have another source of income coming in. Four of us would soon be working and sharing the financial load. I felt less pressure on myself. After 20 years, it was also needed to have the weight distributed away from me as the primary source of income. Although this was a painful period, in looking back, God knew what He was doing. He was preparing us for something unique. We just didn't know what it was yet. Despite this, our faith remained strong. With everyone having a source of income, it was refreshing. This was indeed a different type of family than before.

When I was traveling and being the primary source of income. I missed out on a lot that was going on with the family. Now being home more, I got a chance to delve into things I didn't know about or existed. Many of these things were eye-opening but necessary. Even with the financial situation being a little better, the damage was done psychologically. Those scares were coming out, and at the time, Lisa and I didn't know everything that attributed to it. There was no getting around the fact that if we were to completely get through this season, we needed to continue talking and learning about each other. What was interesting is that God made sure we had what we *needed* and *not* what we *wanted*. This way, *we were forced to confront each other about our issues.*

February 2019 spring classes were going well. I had a smaller class than usual, so I was able to cover a lot of subjects. The students were international baccalaureate students and had GPA averages of 3.25 minimum. I was also enjoying my internship class. This was a different process because I didn't teach them. The internship process was different than a regular course. Many times, I would travel from one job site to another. It was fun interacting with their supervisors. I often received excellent reports about how they were doing. I loved the fact that the employers thought very highly to my students.

Later in the year, I started my new class for the summer of 2019. This was a challenge because it was the first vocational class taught in Rialto, CA. Many students dropped before the course started. By the end of the first week, I had only nine students left. Most of these students had personal issues, but they showed tremendous strength. I was very impressed with them because, despite all the things they were going through, the commitment to finish successfully was evident. I drew strength from their energy, and it renewed my faith. The students finished strong, and I was proud to be their professor, helping them to achieve success.

God had transitioned me from traveling, not being home enough, and being financially comfortable to not traveling, spending time with my family, and living a purposeful life was it always comfortable, no way. I was humbled and broken, but for his purpose and divine will. I have come to learn when a person is led by the Holy Spirit, their life is not their own. I now know I was bought with a price.

Transition through transformation is not easy, but if we keep our eyes on Christ, His grace is sufficient enough for us to endure the potter's wheel and walk into our destiny. 1 Corinthians 6:19-20 says, *"Don't you realize that your body is the temple of the Holy Spirit, who lives in you and was given to you by God? You do not belong to yourself, for God bought you with a high price. So you must honor God with your body."* Finally, 1 Peter 2:21 states, *"For God called you to do good, even if it means suffering, just as Christ suffered or you. He is your example, and you must follow in his steps."*

Reconciliation and change

In February of 2019, one of our key worship leaders left the worship team. This meant there was nobody else strong enough to sing vocal parts for many of the songs we fellowshipped with. I didn't know how we were going to manage this loss, but I had to keep the team going. I knew there would be modifications with Easter quickly approaching, so it was critical to work together and be cohesive. March 2019 was an extension of February 2019.

I was told there was going to be a different type of Good Friday service this year. It was a type of service that is not usually done. However, I was up for the challenge. There were also many changes happening during this period, and for the first time in over 15 years, I felt uneasy. There was too much instability with how the church was being managed that it left me not fully understanding the *real* mission or purpose. June 2019, I made the decision to take time off as the music director. This was a difficult decision, but it was best not only for me but also necessary for our family. This was not an easy decision. I played at our church every week for a year and a half straight, and with everything that was going on financially, the money was needed. However, I wasn't spending enough quality time with the family. This would be the first time in 15 years I wasn't playing on stage, but if my family was to heal, I had to take a break. This decision changed the entire landscape and dynamic of the worship team.

The following month I started looking at other opportunities. Being at one church for 15 years was a blessing, but with this time off, I wanted to grow spiritually, explore my mind, get my weight down, and become a *better man*. If I could be better, it would be better for my family. While Lisa and I were still attending our home church, we were also visiting other churches. It was good to see how different praise team members worship, how other pastors preach, and how other congregations react to the word being taught.

Lisa and I also spent more personal time together. It was great spending time going to the beach, attending concerts, seeing movies, and eating dinner. We spent more time talking about being better people, parents, and relating to each other better. No matter how painful, God wants us to heal, and it took us to be broken. Looking back at it, this was the first time I started to understand *why* I got laid off in 2013. <u>Without the layoff, money would have prevented us from "*pulling back the band-aid to get to the truth*."</u>

August 2019 was the month of understanding. After more than a month of self-reflection, we had a family meeting. At first, I didn't know what to expect. I was hoping for the best, but in the back of my mind, I braced for the worst. When we finally met, many things were discussed. What was also great is that people were apologizing to each other. This turned out to be the first part of real and true reconciliation. When the meeting was over, I was still analyzing everything, but I felt much better about where we were as a family. I now know what the real problems were and what needed to happen to heal. I'm not saying everything was solved immediately, but it was the *first step* in the *right direction.*

Lisa started back to work, teaching at the school district. Two other children were working fulltime jobs. I went back to work, teaching two courses. My youngest was going through the healing process, and my oldest officially moved back to Texas. Lisa and I continued visiting other churches while attending our home church, as well. We received opportunities that would allow us to reach many people for the kingdom.

We eventually found a church that felt good to us. Soon other family members began attending as well. We quickly began serving in the ministry, and we were received well by the church members. I feel like as a family, we turned the page. We still go through issues like everyone else, but *God has, is, and will always have our back*! His grace is good enough, and we have learned to do life, *His way*! Romans 5:1-11 says, *"Therefore, since we have been made right in God's sight by faith, we have peace with God because of what Jesus Christ our Lord has done for us. Because of our faith, Christ has brought us into this place of undeserved privilege where we now stand, and we confidently and joyfully look forward to sharing God's glory. We can rejoice, too, when we run into problems and trials, for we know that they help us develop endurance. And endurance develops strength of character, and character strengthens our confident hope of salvation. And this hope will not lead to disappointment. For we know how dearly God loves us because he has given us the Holy Spirit to fill our hearts with his love. When we were utterly helpless, Christ came at just the right time and died for us sinners. Now, most people would not be willing to die for an upright person, though someone might perhaps be willing to die for a person who is especially good. But God showed his great love for us by sending Christ to die for us while we were still sinners. And since we have been made right in God's sight by the blood of Christ, he will certainly save us from God's condemnation. For since our friendship with God was restored by the death of his Son while we were still his enemies, we will certainly be saved through the life of his Son. So now we can rejoice in our wonderful new relationship with God because our Lord Jesus Christ has made us friends of God."*

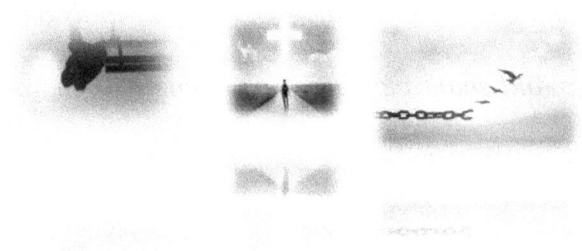

*"The Lord is my strength and shield.
I trust him with all my heart.
He helps me, and my heart is filled with joy.
I burst out in songs of thanksgiving."*
Psalm 28:7

Conclusion

June 2013 through August 2019 has been a time of trials and challenges. There was sickness, death, job loss, personal attacks, and tests, unlike any other time in my life. In looking back, I now honestly believe life is not fair. There was also personal reflection, growth, transition, transformation, and brokenness, which resulted in building stronger faith, having a better understanding of grace, hope, and healing. While this period in my life wasn't comfortable, I believe I've come closer to God's purpose for my life. Without being aligned fully with God's plan for your life, it is not possible to experience God's best. This is not to say things will be easy. I am actually saying quite the opposite. My experience was stressful, draining, scary, and often depressing. I can truthfully say once I began to totally rely on God's strength and not my own, I felt relieved and empowered. I learned that many of the issues and circumstances were out of my control.

Through God's gift of grace, I was able to get through the challenges of life. I also learned I was responsible for my job, and *I could not do God's job.* This was a critical but necessary lesson to grow into a close relationship with God. It is imperative to have a close relationship with God to live with purpose based on God's best. We can begin to realize God's best by understanding His will. This can be done by pursuing to know God. If we seek God's will before putting Him first, we put ourselves in control rather than allowing the Holy Spirit to lead us. This can be dangerous. Separating the pursuit of God's will without knowing Him, prevents us from staying on *His* course of events. We should know God and his word *first* before we can ask Him to reveal His purpose and direction in our lives. We must have a love for God and what *He loves.* This will require us to perform a self-analysis and ask ourselves, do we *really* want to know God? Once we are in alignment with God's purpose, we have to trust in Him and His ability to work in our lives. This means letting go and turn the reigns over to the Lord, *regardless* of the situation.

We must also continue to pray daily and ask the Holy Spirit for wisdom. Matthew 7:7-8 says, *"Ask, and it will be given to you; seek, and you will find; knock, and the door will be opened to you. For everyone who asks receives; the one who seeks finds; and to the one who knocks, the door will be opened."*

Finally, we must wait for God to act and not get ahead of him or take things upon ourselves in our own strength. This level of discipline requires building up our faith in God's word. Standing on the word of God many times is not easy but required. 1 Corinthians 16:13 says, *"Be on guard. Stand firm in the faith. Be courageous. Be strong."* 1 Corinthians 15:58 says, *"So, my dear brothers and sisters, be strong and immovable. Always work enthusiastically for the Lord, for you know that nothing you do for the Lord is ever useless."* Finally, Ephesians 6:11 states, *"Put on all of God's armor so that you will be able to stand firm against all strategies of the devil."*

Transitioning into a different phase of life doesn't have to be a negative experience if we understand who we are and who God is. We must love Him enough to submit to His guidance and leadership, stay in daily prayer, and stand on God's word by faith. I pray for all of you that your transition is successful, purposeful, and above all, be aligned with God's plan for your life!

References

1 Corinthians 6:19 Do you not know that your body is a .... https://biblehub.com/1_corinthians/6-19.htm

1 Corinthians 9:27 NLT - I discipline my body like an .... https://www.biblegateway.com/passage/?search=1+Corinthians+9%3A27&version=NLT

1 John 3:1 Behold what manner of love the Father has given .... https://www.biblehub.com/1_john/3-1.htm

1 Peter 4:12-13 ESV - Suffering as a Christian - Beloved .... https://www.biblegateway.com/passage/?search=1+Peter+4%3A12-13&version=ESV

1 Peter 1:7 - NLT - These trials will show that your faith https://www.biblestudytools.com/nlt/1-peter/1-7.html

II Timothy 1:7 For God has not given us a spirit of fear https://www.bible.com/bible/114/2TI.1.7.nkjv

2 Corinthians 3:18 And we all, with unveiled face https://www.bible.com/bible/59/2CO.3.18.esv

20 Bible Verses & Healing Scriptures that Only God Can Give. https://www.ibelieve.com/faith/20-bible-verses-about-healing-that-only-god-can-give.html

25 Inspirational Bible Verses About Boldness. http://biblereasons.com/boldness/

100+ Best Funeral Quotes | Love Lives On. https://www.loveliveson.com/100-funeral-quotes/

About Us | Bridge Radio. https://www.bridgeradio.org/about-us/

Albrecht, Tamara. "Tools for Finding Your Way Through Conflicts." The American Organist, vol. 49, no. 3, American Guild of Organists, Mar. 2015, p. 77.

Bible Gateway. (2019) Retrieved from https://www.biblegateway.com/

Bible Story of Job (2019) Retrieved from https://www.biblestudytools.com/bible-stories/bible-story-of-job.html

Bible Study Tools. (2019) Retrieved from https://www.biblestudytools.com/nlt/passage/?q=psalm+27;+psalm+9

Charles Kelly | Scores | CD Baby Music Store. https://store.cdbaby.com/cd/charleskelly13

Dashing Devotional: Fighting for Your Health | Blog .... https://www.dashingdish.com/blog/fighting-for-your-health

Deuteronomy 8:3 He humbled you, and in your hunger He gave https://biblehub.com/deuteronomy/8-3.htm

Deuteronomy 26, New Living Translation (NLT) | The Bible App. https://www.bible.com/bible/116/DEU.26.nlt

Ephesians 6:13 NLT: Therefore, put on every piece of God's https://biblehub.com/nlt/ephesians/6-13.htm

Exodus 15:26 - He said, "If you listen carefully to the https://www.biblestudytools.com/exodus/15-26.html

Hebrews 12, New Living Translation (NLT) | The Bible App. https://www.bible.com/bible/116/HEB.12.nlt

Hebrews 12:1 Therefore, since we are surrounded by such a https://www.biblehub.com/hebrews/12-1.htm

Hebrews 12:28 Since we are receiving a Kingdom that is.... https://www.biblegateway.com/passage/?search=Hebrews%2012:28

Heeren, J. (2019). Bible Study Tools. Retrieved from https://www.biblestudytools.com/bible-study/topical-studies/six-beautiful-ways-to-understand-gods-grace.html

Institutional Review Board | University of Phoenix .... https://research.phoenix.edu/content/institutional-review-board

Isaiah 46:9-10 - NLT - Remember the things I have done in .... https://www.biblestudytools.com/nlt/isaiah/passage/?q=isaiah+46:9-10

Isaiah 46:10 NLT: Only I can tell you the future before it https://biblehub.com/nlt/isaiah/46-10.htm

Isaiah 55:8 NLT: "My thoughts are nothing like your https://www.biblehub.com/nlt/isaiah/55-8.htm

Isaiah 55:9 "For as the heavens are higher than the earth https://biblehub.com/isaiah/55-9.htm

Isaiah 55:10 NLT: "The rain and snow come down from the https://biblehub.com/nlt/isaiah/55-10.htm

James 1:2-18 - NLT - Dear brothers and sisters, when .... https://www.biblestudytools.com/nlt/james/passage/?q=james+1:2-18

Jeremiah 17:5-8 This is what the LORD says: "Cursed are https://www.bible.com/bible/116/JER.17.5-8.nlt

Jeremiah 30:18 NLT: This is what the LORD says: "When I https://biblehub.com/nlt/jeremiah/30-18.htm

Jeremiah 30 (NLT) - The LORD gave another message. https://www.blueletterbible.org/nlt/jer/30/1/s_775001

Jeremiah 30:17-20 NLT - I will give you back your health .... https://www.biblegateway.com/passage/?search=Jeremiah+30%3A17-20&version=NLT

Jeremiah 30:20-22 NLT - Their children will prosper as .... https://www.biblegateway.com/passage/?search=Jeremiah+30%3A20-22&version=NLT

Jeremiah 1:5 "Before I formed you in the womb I knew you https://www.biblehub.com/jeremiah/1-5.htm

John 16:33 I have told you these things so that in Me you https://biblehub.com/john/16-33.htm

Knock and the Door Will Be Opened - FaithGateway. https://www.faithgateway.com/knock-door-opened/

Learning How to Pray for Boldness - Milk and Honey Faith. https://www.milkandhoneyfaith.com/2019/07/pray-for-boldness-2.html/

Luke 12:23 For life is more than food, and the body more https://www.biblehub.com/luke/12-23.htm

Luke 3:11 - Bible Gateway. https://www.biblegateway.com/verse/en/Luke%203%3A11

Matthew 7:13 NLT: "You can enter God's Kingdom only https://biblehub.com/nlt/matthew/7-13.htm

Matthew 7:14 But small is the gate and narrow the way that https://biblehub.com/matthew/7-14.htm

Matthew 25:40 - Bible Gateway. https://www.biblegateway.com/verse/en/Matthew%2025%3A40

Matthew 6:25-34 NLT - "That is why I tell you not to worry .... https://www.biblegateway.com/passage/?search=Matthew%206:25-34&version=NLT

Motl, A. (2019). How Do We Know God's Will for Our Lives? Retrieved from https://www.christianity.com/wiki/christian-life/how-do-we-know-god-s-will-for-our-lives.html

Nehemiah 6:9 - They were all trying to frighten us https://www.biblestudytools.com/nehemiah/6-9.html

Psalm 27 KJV; NLT - The LORD is my light and my salvation .... https://www.biblegateway.com/passage/?search=Psalm+27&version=KJV;NLT

Psalm 27 KJV; NLT - The LORD is my light and my salvation .... https://www.biblegateway.com/passage/?search=Psalm+27&version=KJV;NLT

Psalm 27:4 - NLT - The one thing I ask of the LORD — the https://www.biblestudytools.com/nlt/psalms/27-4.html

Psalms 27:4-6 Here's the one thing I crave from God, the https://www.bible.com/bible/compare/PSA.27.4-6

Psalm 27 KJV; NLT - The LORD is my light and my salvation .... https://www.biblegateway.com/passage/?search=Psalm+27&version=KJV;NLT

Psalm 27:10-14 - NLT - Even if my father and mother .... https://www.biblestudytools.com/nlt/psalms/passage/?q=psalm+27:10-14

Psalm 84:11 For the LORD God is a sun and a shield; the https://biblehub.com/psalms/84-11.htm

Psalm 91:1 - NLT - Those who live in the shelter of the https://www.biblestudytools.com/nlt/psalms/91-1.html

Psalm 91 Prayer of Protection and Hedge of Protection Prayer. https://www.missionariesofprayer.org/2010/11/psalm-91-prayer-hedge-protection/

Psalms 91 NLT - Psalm 91 - Those who live in the - Bible .... https://www.biblegateway.com/passage/?search=psalms%2091&version=NLT

Psalm 91:4 He will cover you with His feathers; under His https://www.biblehub.com/psalms/91-4.htm

Psalm 118:24 This is the day.... https://www.biblegateway.com/passage/?search=Psalm+118%3A24&version=NLT

Pray and Let God Worry - Harvest.
https://harvest.org/resources/devotion/pray-and-let-god-worry/

Research Participants (2019) – JCHR - jaeb.org.
https://www.jaeb.org/research-participants/

RMW 2018 Stronger Theme - YouTube.
https://www.youtube.com/watch?v=CohCeE99_ak

Rom 8:29 Cross References (33 Verses).
https://www.openbible.info/labs/cross-references/search?q=Romans+8%3A29

Romans 5:5-11 And this hope will not lead to ....
https://www.bible.com/bible/116/ROM.5.5-11.nlt

Romans 5:6 NLT: When we were utterly helpless, Christ came https://biblehub.com/nlt/romans/5-6.htm

Romans 12:12 NLT: Rejoice in our confident hope....
https://www.biblegateway.com/passage/?search=Romans+12%3A12&version=NLT

Scriptures and the Spiritual Gift of Healing.
https://www.learnreligions.com/spiritual-gift-of-healing-712476

SoundsOfSunrise - Home | Facebook.
https://www.facebook.com/SoundsOfSunrise-191933887492990/

SoundsOfSunrise - "Runaway" - YouTube.
https://www.youtube.com/watch?v=KtRHdM4bF38

Smith, S. (2019). OpenBible.info Retrieved from https://www.openbible.info/topics/standing_firm_in_your_faith

The Lord Will Fight for You - 9 Reminders from God's Word https://www.crosswalk.com/blogs/debbie-mcdaniel/when-life-is-hard-9-reminders-that-god-fights-for-us.html

The Stress Cure - Proverbs 31.
https://proverbs31.org/read/devotions/full-post/2014/09/24/the-stress-cure

The Supernatural Stream of Peace Sermon by Dean Courtier https://www.sermoncentral.com/sermons/the-supernatural-stream-of-peace-dean-courtier-sermon-on-peace-with-god-195830

The Promises of God: 10 Powerful Bible Verses.
https://www.whatchristianswanttoknow.com/the-promises-of-god-10-powerful-bible-verses-1/

Washington, James. "Check out Paul." The Triangle Tribune, vol. 17, no. 56, Charlotte Post Publishing Co., 1 May 2016, p. 8A.

What does the Bible Say About Worry? - learnreligions.com. https://www.learnreligions.com/what-does-the-bible-say-about-worry-701994

What does Ephesians 6 mean? - BibleRef.com. https://www.bibleref.com/Ephesians/6/Ephesians-chapter-6.html

What does John 16:13 mean? - Online Bible Commentary. https://www.bibleref.com/John/16/John-16-13.html

What does the Bible Say About Complaining? A Christian Study. https://www.whatchristianswanttoknow.com/what-does-the-bible-say-about-complaining-a-christian-study/

What does Philippians 1:6 mean? - BibleRef.com. https://www.bibleref.com/Philippians/1/Philippians-1-6.html

What does Revelation 21:4 mean? - BibleRef.com. https://www.bibleref.com/Revelation/21/Revelation-21-4.html

What is the peace of God, and how can I experience it .... https://www.gotquestions.org/peace-of-God.html

When Nothing's Going Right - Proverbs 31 Ministries. https://proverbs31.org/read/devotions/full-post/2016/02/04/when-nothings-going-right

https://pixabay.com/photos/water-nature-sea-travel-landscape-3166432/

Image by Gerd Altmann from Pixabay - https://pixabay.com/photos/religion-faith-cross-light-hand-3717899/

Image by Peggy und Marco Lachmann-Anke from Pixabay https://pixabay.com/illustrations/breakthrough-wall-opening-1027872/

Image by Pete Linforth from Pixabay - https://pixabay.com/illustrations/binary-map-internet-technology-1012756/

Image by Igor Link from Pixabay - https://pixabay.com/photos/success-business-woman-career-jump-2697951/

Image by kordula vahle from Pixabay - https://pixabay.com/photos/beach-north-sea-sea-sunset-water-2179624/

Image by Patricia Alexandre from Pixabay - https://pixabay.com/photos/nature-outdoor-sky-cloud-cloudy-3294543/

Image by Noupload from Pixabay - https://pixabay.com/illustrations/robot-technology-2033898/

Image by John Hain from Pixabay - https://pixabay.com/illustrations/man-standing-qualities-thanking-1207675/

Image by Andrew Martin from Pixabay - https://pixabay.com/photos/rest-thankful-peace-thanks-quiet-1392482/

Photo by freestocks.org from Pexels - https://www.pexels.com/photo/christmas-tree-with-baubles-717988/

Winston Churchill Quotes - https://www.brainyquote.com/search_results?q=the+price+of+greatness+is+responsibility

Image by Gerd Altmann from Pixabay - https://pixabay.com/photos/religion-faith-cross-light-hand-3717899/

Image by John Hain from Pixabay - https://pixabay.com/illustrations/alive-awake-aware-secure-open-1250975/

Image by Gerd Altmann from Pixabay - https://pixabay.com/illustrations/faith-love-hope-wave-clouds-sea-4411141/

Image by Gerd Altmann from Pixabay - https://pixabay.com/illustrations/predator-tiger-man-fear-view-2217941/

Image by Alexas_Fotos from Pixabay - https://pixabay.com/photos/do-not-give-up-motivation-live-2015253/

Image by charlotte_202003 from Pixabay - https://pixabay.com/photos/bible-christian-jesus-religion-2989425/

About the Author

Dr. Charles Anderson Kelly was born on October 22, 1957, in Philadelphia, Pennsylvania, and currently resides in Rialto, California. Charles is an innovative professional with more than 20 years of experience as a successful business owner, SAP preferred partner, project manager, consultant, instructor, and developer for Business Objects, Sales and Distribution, Governance Risk & Compliance, and Retail software modules worldwide. Charles has worked as a senior consultant in the Semi-Conductor, Retail, Technology, Insurance, Automotive, Medical, Music/Entertainment, Government, Energy, Pharmaceutical and Manufacturing, and Non-Profit (Education and Religious) industries. Charles is also a gold record (RIAA, BMI) musician/keyboardist, record producer, film composer, music director, and songwriter. He has worked with Stevie Wonder, Neil Diamond, Elton John, Sister Sledge, The Pointer Sisters, Debbie Allen, Nathan Watts, Paul Jackson Jr., The Walt Disney Company, and many others. He also was an actor in the TV series "Fame." From the years 2005 through June of 2019, Charles was the Music Director for one of the largest churches in Southern California and is currently serving as the keyboardist for the largest megachurch in the city of Highland, California. Charles also earned a Bachelor of Science degree in Information Technology in 2006, a master's in Business Administration in 2012, and a doctorate in Business Administration in 2017.

To contact the author write:
Dr. Charles A Kelly
909-356-0800
Internet Address:
Charles.Kelly@soundsofsunrise.com

Please let me know how this book has helped you in your personal journey. I want to wish you well and may God bless you in your transition towards purposeful living.

www.ingramcontent.com/pod-product-compliance
Lightning Source LLC
Chambersburg PA
CBHW070850050426
42453CB00012B/2119